PAINTED FURNITURE

Simple Techniques for Fresh, New Looks

Diane M. Weaver

Sterling Publishing Co., Inc.
New York
A STERLING/LARK BOOK

To the memory of my father, Gay C. LaRose, who loved to paint furniture any number of ways and often did, and to the creative inspiration and encouragement of my mother, Helen.

Editor: Leslie Dierks
Design: Kathleen Holmes
Photo art direction and styling: Diane Weaver
Photography: Richard Babb
Production: Elaine Thompson and Kathleen Holmes

Library of Congress Cataloging-in-Publication Data

Weaver, Diane, M.. 1949–
Painted furniture : simple techniques for fresh, new looks / Diane M. Weaver.
p. cm.
"A Sterling/Lark book."
Includes index.
ISBN 0-8069-0839-4
1. Furniture finishing. 2. Furniture painting. I. Title.
TT199.4.W4 1995
749--dc20 94-22524
CIP

10 9 8

A Sterling/Lark Book

First paperback edition published in 1995 by
Sterling Publishing Company, Inc.
387 Park Avenue South, New York, N.Y. 10016

Produced by Altamont Press, Inc.
50 College Street, Asheville, NC 28801

Distributed in Canada by Sterling Publishing
% Canadian Manda Group, One Atlantic Avenue, Suite 105
Toronto, Ontario, Canada M6K 3E7

Distributed in Great Britain and Europe by Cassell PLC
Wellington House, 125 Strand, London WC2R 0BB, England

Distributed in Australia by Capricorn Link (Australia) Pty Ltd.
P.O. Box 6651, Baulkham Hills, Business Centre, NSW 2153, Australia

Sterling ISBN 0-8069-0839-4 Trade
0-8069-0840-8 Paper

A Note to the Reader

Joy, I'm convinced, is that heart-filling emotion that results from an involvement in creative activities. Every last one of us has the capacity for experiencing joy in life, but in varying amounts. Some of us must create cities, some must invent a new recipe, and some must cause mayhem all in our own way to achieve our level of joyous satisfaction. Joy is what inspires me to paint. Joy is what I hope you will attain as you read and use this book.

It's important to study and learn from what others have conceived, but the essence and excitement of creation comes from being able to say, "I did it my way." That is the spirit with which I encourage you to read, interpret, and practice what you find in this book.

Try to relax and have fun while you're pursuing your creativity. This book will help eliminate the frustration of not knowing how to approach a project, and it will show how to solve the technical problems involved. My goal in writing it has been to provide you with enough information so that you can enjoy yourself, but not so much that you are robbed of the chance to make your own discoveries. Pursue the fun, relax, and enJoy.

Acknowledgments

Special thanks—to my husband, Dick, for all of his patience and help.

to Liz and Pete Sullivan, who graciously shared their 20 years of professional knowledge and gave freely of their time and advice.

and to their daughter, Lisa, whose help in painting several of the projects was greatly appreciated.

to the Hinman family for the use of their beautiful home and grounds to photograph several of the projects.

to the Barnes family for the use of their playhouse.

to Amy and Rick Texido and their dog Sydney.

to Edd and Peg Elkins Antiques.

to the Applebaum family.

to Stephens Upholstery.

"…there is a way to stop the rampant spread of beauty. It has to do with regimentation, conformity, assembly line aesthetics, and the triumph of the functional over the haphazard."

Anne Rice
The Tale of the Body Thief

CONTENTS

Introduction

No matter what home decorating magazine you open today, you'll find painted furniture somewhere inside. From traditional to contemporary, country to Victorian, all will reveal pictures of furnishings with painted finishes. Interest in the painted surface continues to grow; not only magazines, but newspapers, galleries, and furniture showrooms also reflect the trend.

Many of the periodicals tell where the painted pieces are available and at what prices. The prices always stick in your mind, and they're often well out of reach for the average homeowner. Is there another alternative? Could you paint similar pieces yourself?

The general public, with its new and improved attitude that says, "I can do it," is beginning to understand that producing a piece of painted furniture with professional-looking results isn't out of the question. The do-it-yourself kits that demonstrate the simplicity of painting faux marble or granite are partly responsible. The kits, however, wouldn't be successful if it weren't for the development of convenient paints.

The selection of craft acrylic paints available to home hobbyists has exploded in recent years. Almost any color is available ready for use, premixed, from a wide variety of manufacturers, and at a reasonable price. To complete the picture, easy-to-use polyurethane varnish makes these paints practical for many applications. The soft acrylic surface can be protected with an easily applied, fast-drying coat of varnish that will stand up to the attacks of everyday family life. These materials are also environmentally safe, quick drying, and convenient to clean up with water.

Not all of the projects in this book are done with water-based paints, though. For some faux finishes, the classic oil-based materials produce better results, and the difference is great enough to warrant their use. Don't be discouraged from trying these projects. An apparent disadvantage of oil-based paint—such as a longer drying time—can turn to your advantage when you're rendering rosewood or reworking a marble vein.

The projects in this book will help you to explore the use of new materials plus some of the more traditional ones. You'll learn classic and innovative ways of producing time-honored effects, and you'll find some new textures and images that will expand your bag of tricks for decorative painting. These projects are designed to be within the grasp of the beginner, yet still challenge the accomplished hobbyist or artist.

Before You Begin

Selecting an interesting piece of furniture that will finish well may take a bit of imagination. Some wooden hulks look as though they're beyond hope, as did the projects on pages 25 and 126. Some oddities, ugly in their original clothes, whisper their delightful possibilities into our subconscious, igniting our desires. When they're finished, these pieces usually give us the greatest pleasure of all.

If you intend to buy a piece of used furniture and don't want to make a lot of repairs, check for sturdiness. Some chairs that appear all right except for "that crack" can't be repaired without replacing major sections. This is particularly true of rockers. In addition to looking for potential mechanical problems, search for insect damage.

Look carefully at the exterior of your chosen piece. If you want to strip and refinish the wood, look for attractive, even color and grain. This can be difficult to determine when there are 15 layers of paint slathered on the entire object. You may have to reserve your final decision on how to refinish a particular piece until it has had time to reveal itself.

If you're considering a dresser or cabinet, inspect the inside of the drawers. Are these boxes sturdy and still useful? You may not want to rebuild an entire set of drawers just because you liked the squiggly design or the veneer on the drawer front.

Look for a type of wood that will accommodate your chosen finish most easily. For example, a lacquer finish over oak calls for a lot of filling and priming to smooth the grain, and this translates into time, elbow grease, and a dedication to perfection far beyond that achieved by most mortals. Paradoxically, a smooth, soft-grained pine game table would also be a poor choice because the soft wood would dent easily, destroying your perfect finish.

Don't limit your selection to wood. Metal (see the file cabinet on page 64), wicker, rattan, resin, or plastic are all good possibilities. Even terra cotta (see page 38) or the back side of a glass table top can be painted. A faux finish, such as a totally elegant marble, on an old galvanized bucket may be just what your otherwise formal library needs, and it makes a good trompe l'oeil joke.

Purchasing an inexpensive piece of well-designed and sturdily built used furniture that was mass produced in the 1920s or later may prove to be the best choice for adding a new finish. You won't have to invest too much money, and you'll usually find attractive, good quality woods and veneers under all of those coats of paint.

Don't paint a serious antique no matter how little it cost you or how much the original color clashes with your sofa. Some older or antique pieces may be great finds that look to the unpracticed eye as though they need a coat of mauve paint, and well they may. If you have any questions about the true value of a piece of furniture, ask an expert. Sell it if you don't like the color, and buy something else. Painting it would only devalue a piece of furniture that can't be replaced.

The charming, handmade, antique American country high chair shown here is a good example of what not to paint. It still has a considerable amount of its original green paint. Removing any of this paint or painting over the aged patina would greatly reduce its value.

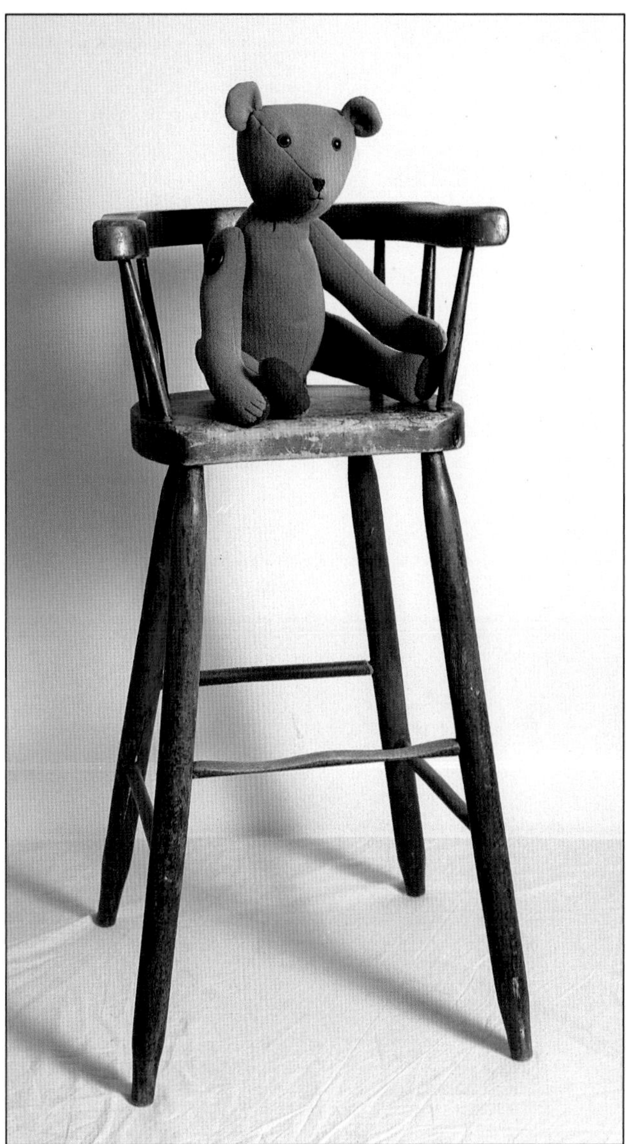

Restoring paint is another project altogether and is done to enhance the value of an antique that can't be appreciated in its time-worn state. The flat-to-the-wall, step-back cupboard on page 126 is an excellent example of a cabinet whose dilapidated condition demands repair or the mercy of the tinder box. That project reveals how experts Liz and Pete Sullivan snatched a worthwhile piece from the junk barn just in time.

Of course, you can avoid "old stuff" by buying newly manufactured unfinished furniture. There are some distinct advantages to this approach. A piece with the right size, shape, and style for your particular need is usually available without too much hunting, and you can choose different types of wood and, sometimes, detailing options to customize it. Unfortunately, the quality of the piece in the showroom may not match that of the delivered product. It's best to look over your custom-manufactured piece of furniture in the bright light of the showroom before accepting it in your home. After waiting several months for a piece to arrive at your home, it's difficult to remain calm as you give the unsuspecting delivery person the option of replacing a warped board or returning your deposit *now.*

Selecting a piece of furniture to paint, the method and style of decoration, and the end use are all tied together. You wouldn't select a bucket bench out of a barn, grain it with faux rosewood, and position the miscreation in your Louis XV parlor. Or would you? Keep your dreams in mind when you make your choices.

The Preparation Process

Preparing a piece of furniture for painting or refinishing is often more important than painting the finish itself. No amount of paint or varnish will cover a poor job of sanding or an inferior priming coat. A wave of wood filler that wasn't properly sanded and sealed can't be disguised with multiple coats of paint and varnish, no matter how much you sand each layer. It's best to do the job right if you're going to do it at all.

Removing all of the old finish before starting a new one may not be necessary. If you're going to use paint, and the existing finish is sound and fairly smooth, you need to sand the surface only enough to remove the shine, making the surface rough enough to bond with the new paint. Test the old finish to see how well it's bonded to the underlying surface by pressing a 3-inch (7.6 cm) or longer piece of masking tape firmly onto the old finish and removing it with a quick, ripping motion. If the finish holds, it doesn't need to be removed.

Before painting a finish that begs to be touched, such as this faux rosewood, sand your project until it's perfectly smooth.

Sanding

Before you begin to sand a previously painted surface, it's important for health reasons to know whether or not the finish contains lead. Most interior furniture is unlikely to have been finished with paint containing lead in more than a trace amount. Tinted, over-the-counter paints made through the 1960s contained trace amounts of lead, and industrial yellow safety paint still does. The real danger from paint containing toxic amounts of lead was created in the 1930s and 1940s, when house painters added lead pigment to exterior paints to increase the coverage and durability of their finishes. Bird houses and garden furniture were the most likely candidates to receive this heavily leaded exterior house paint.

Lead, even in small amounts, is hazardous, and the tiny particles freed by sanding are difficult, if not impossible, to vacuum away. If you're unsure about the lead content of any paint finish (clear finishes contain no lead), check the paint with a household lead-testing kit. You can find these at most paint stores or paint departments. If the test reveals the presence of lead, don't sand your project. Applying a commercial stripper, although not totally safe, is a far safer method than sanding lead paint.

Abrasive paper, commonly called sandpaper, can be made from any number of gritty substances. The two types most often used for the projects in this book are garnet and silicon carbide (also called wet/dry sandpaper). Experiment with these and some others to find which works best for you. Garnet paper can be used on bare wood or on surfaces that have been varnished or painted. Wet/dry sandpaper, as its name suggests, can be used dry on bare wood and wet over paint or varnish. The advantage of using it wet is that you're less likely to create fine scratches in your surface. When using the paper wet, first mix a little soap and water to make suds. Pat the suds onto your surface with a damp sponge; then sand. Rinse with clear water, and pat the wood dry with a soft towel. Then use a tack rag to remove any residue of dust.

All types of sandpaper are sold in various grades ranging from coarse to extra fine. Start with the coarser, and work to the finer ones. The finer the grade of paper used to prepare the surface, the finer the ultimate finish will be.

Large pieces of furniture can be prepared quickly with an electric power sander and garnet paper, progressing from medium- to fine-grade paper. This will raise plenty of dust, so wear a dust mask, and if possible, work outdoors. When using an electric sander, keep the machine in motion to avoid scarring the wood. Sand smaller pieces by hand, starting with medium- and ending with fine-grade sandpaper. Use smaller pieces of paper to get into corners and other tight places. Whether sanding by hand or with electric tools, always sand bare wood in the direction of the grain.

Creating a finish that you can be proud of also requires scrupulous sanding between each application of primer, base coat, paint, and varnish. On flat surfaces, use a sanding block when sanding by hand, and make long, firm, even strokes back and forth. Unless otherwise directed in the project, sand across the brush strokes of the finish. On sharp edges, sand with a much lighter touch. Sand without a block on uneven surfaces and relief carvings, again using a lighter, more sensitive touch. A convex surface can be sanded with the paper wrapped around it to form a cuff.

The degree of smoothness needed on your project is related to the type of finish you desire. A faux marquetry or lacquer finish requires a surface that is silky smooth, but a combed or textured finish isn't so demanding. If you have a smooth, bare piece of wood, you don't need to sand it until after it's been primed because priming will raise the grain.

Stripping

Whenever using commercial stripping compounds, protect your hands by wearing rubber gloves. Wear eye goggles or safety glasses to protect your eyes from spatters.

With the flat side of a stiff bristle brush, apply a thickness of about 1/4 inch (6 mm) of the stripper onto your piece of furniture. Following the manufacturer's directions, wait the recommended time; then remove the wrinkling paint with a putty knife, steel wool, and old rags. Rinse. When the surface is dry, sand it first with the medium-grade paper, then with the fine paper until the surface is suitable for the planned finish.

Store stripper and all other solvents in a safe place away from heat, where children can't get into them. Always observe all of the manufacturers' precautions. Read the labels before you purchase a solvent to make sure that it's the right stripper for the job, and always use the mildest solvent available for the task involved.

Caustic sodas and methylene chloride dips are very popular for the quick removal of paint. This is best done by experts. The caustic soda is considered a "hot dip," since the soda solution must be heated for it to work. Use it only in desperate circumstances and not on veneer. It's not recommended for use on oak, cherry, and walnut due to the damage it causes the wood. It may split and darken mahogany, cherry, and walnut. Caustic soda must be washed off with water and, to neutralize it, oxalic acid. This in turn must be thoroughly washed away with water, or it will leave a crystal deposit on the stripped wood. Caustic soda also eats away the glue and loosens the joints. Methylene chloride is known as a "cold dip," since no heat is involved. The wood is submerged into a mixture of methylene chloride and other paint solvents that are found in most strippers. It's more expensive than caustic soda, but it's far less damaging.

Don't pour solvents down sink drains or into the toilet. Dispose of solvents at a local government hazardous waste station. When doing so, keep solvents in their original containers, properly labeled. Transport them with caution. If there is no local hazardous waste facility, contact a chemical reprocessing plant to take them.

Rags or steel wool soaked in solvents should be allowed to air dry; then dispose of them in the household trash. Don't clean the rags in your washing machine.

An elegant faux finish, such as marble, will fool the eye more successfully if the underlying surface is flawless.

Filling

Depending on the degree of smoothness desired in the final finish, flaws, holes, cracks, and other breaks in the uniformity of a surface may need filling.

Rock-hard water putty is a plasterlike mix that is good for filling cracks and other deep flaws in interior surfaces in wood. Following the manufacturer's directions, use a putty knife to fill the flaw slightly more than full (this is called "filling proud"). Allow the putty to dry; then sand it level, and seal it with shellac. Water-based wood putties tend to shrink and crack over time, but they're convenient and easy to use in many situations. For example, putty can also be used for making molds to replace the missing curlicues on a cabinet. See page 72.

Plastic wood filler isn't as easy to work with, but it forms a harder surface than water-based putty does. It's good for filling chips and small imperfections. Read and follow the manufacturer's instructions.

Sealing

Knots and old stains must be sealed before a piece of furniture is primed and painted. Some primers are formulated to include a sealer. Otherwise, a coat of shellac over bare wood will seal the knots and stains and prevent them from seeping through and ruining the final finish. Shellac is either orange—unbleached—or clear—bleached. Never shake, but always stir shellac. Agitating the shellac creates bubbles that will dry as imperfections in the surface. Additionally, never apply shellac in damp weather. The dampness will cause a milky cloud to appear on the surface. Keep a special brush just for shellac, and clean it with denatured alcohol. If the bristles become stiff, clean them first with ammonia, then with water. Never use soap on your shellac brush.

Priming

Most of the painted projects in this book call for a primer coat. The primer fills and seals, and it provides bonding agents between the bare wood and the next layer of paint. Primer should be applied across the grain of the wood, allowed to dry, then sanded smooth with fine paper. Follow the manufacturer's suggestions on drying time. If a second coat is required, lightly sand between coats to remove any brush marks, hair, or other debris, and apply the next coat across the first. Tinting your primer to make it the same color as your top coat or base coat will save time and money, and it may eliminate the need for a base coat altogether.

Acrylic primer is an all-purpose primer that dries fast and sands smooth. Let it cure well, and sand it before applying an oil-based finish over it. If you don't allow enough time for it to dry hard, acrylic primer has a tendency to roll up when you sand it. Acrylic water-based primer, although convenient, is really best used only when a hard, durable finish is *not* required. An acrylic base coat will allow even a hard oil-based finish to dent easily, especially when applied on soft wood such as pine. If you're producing a distressed finish, then dents aren't a problem, and the convenience of the acrylic makes it the better choice. When applied on metal, water-based acrylics must be sealed with a final top coat that isn't water based.

White pigmented shellac fills, seals, and dries fast, and it sands to an extremely smooth finish. The application of white shellac can take a little bit of getting used to because it's thick. The thickness causes considerable drag on the brush, but the end result is worth the trouble. Use it for finer finishes and when a hard finish is needed under oil-based paint. Shellac works equally well under water-based paints. The added advantage to this material is that it fills the grain and small flaws in the surface. With each added layer, it continues to fill flaws. Sand it between coats to produce a completely smooth surface. When you're finished, clean your brushes and other painting equipment with ammonia. Do not use foam applicators with shellac.

Oil-based primer goes on smoothly and provides a tough surface for overpainting. Use it on finished pieces that will be subjected to wear and tear. Exterior-grade oil primer may be necessary for furniture that will live outdoors. Do not apply any oil-based primers or paints with a foam applicator.

Traditional gesso is a mixture made from white pigment and a binder such as glue. It's best when applied on a rigid surface because it may crack when flexed. Apply the first coat, thinned first with water, allow it to dry, and sand lightly. Then repeat with a second, full-strength coat.

Acrylic polymer gesso has the flexibility that traditional gesso doesn't and is applied the same way. I recommend using the acrylic gesso, especially when painting unglazed terra-cotta surfaces.

This headboard was already stained and varnished when the owner decided to add a bright flower garland adapted from the fabric pillow. The finished surface was prepared by sanding the old varnish in the design area with several very small pieces of #400 paper and a little soapy water. To remove any wax and to prepare the old varnish to bond with the final layer of semigloss polyurethane, the entire surface of the board was then smoothed first with a medium, then with a fine grade of steel wool. The sanding was done with caution to avoid disturbing the stain color.

The design outline was then traced onto the headboard, and a coat of gesso was applied as a primer inside the outline of the design. The gesso not only acts as a binder, but the clear, white ground also allows the acrylic colors of the garland to show their brightest.

Tools and Materials

In today's market, there is a wide selection of decorative painting tools suitable for amateurs. The popularity of do-it-yourself painting has created such a demand that even grocery stores are selling stenciling and marbling kits. With all the manufacturers rushing to meet this demand, there are many versions of the same tool accessible in every price range. No matter what type of brush or implement you need to complete a project successfully, it's readily obtainable.

Brushes

Paintbrushes come in an array of natural and manmade bristles and are held together by a metal ferrule that is fastened to a handle. The free end of the bristles is called the tip of the brush, and where the bristles and ferrule meet is called the heel. Brushes vary greatly in quality and suitability. Buy the best one that you can afford for the job because there is a tremendous difference in performance between a good brush and a cheap one.

Brushes are the most important tool of this craft, so treat them well. Brush care is especially important when you consider the money that you have invested in even a small collection. To clean a brush, start by wiping the excess paint onto a rag; then continue cleaning it with the appropriate solution of mineral spirits, silicone brush cleaner, or mild soap and water. Acetone, paint solvent, shellac remover, or lacquer thinner shouldn't be used to clean a brush because they can dissolve the gluing agents that hold the brush together. Finish the cleaning of a good brush with a cleaner and conditioner. Don't leave a brush sitting on its tip, soaking, or the bristles will be permanently bent, and the wood handle will swell and cause the ferrule to loosen. Dry your brush away from heaters. To avoid damaging the bristles, mix your paint with a pallet knife, not a paintbrush. Don't dip a dry, natural hair brush directly into paint; wet it first.

When choosing brushes for your projects, you'll find that there is considerable variety in the material used to make the bristles. Several of the most common—and those most likely to be needed for the projects in this book—are described here.

Bristle brushes are made from hog hair. The bristles are white or light in color and are used with oils and acrylics. The bristles are stiff and usually untrimmed on the ends, where the bristle hair splits into a "V" at the tip. This split tip is called a flag, and it helps the brush to carry paint and maintain its shape. Brushes are assembled with the natural curve of the bristles facing inward so that the flag tips interlock, helping the brush maintain its spring, shape, and control.

Ox hairs from the ears of oxen are strong and springy and have tapering points. Ox hair is used alone in a brush or sometimes combined with other hair. Ox-hair brushes are suitable for oil- and water-based paints and for shellac.

Red sable brushes, made from the hair on the tail of a marten, are golden or red in color. Sable is soft yet resilient, allowing for maximum control. Red sable brushes are used for both oil and water media.

Badger hair is soft and springy and natural in color. Brushes made from badger hair can be used for both oil- and water-based media.

Squirrel is soft and absorbent, but it has little spring when it's wet. Squirrel-hair brushes are good for applying smooth painted finishes.

Natural and synthetic blends are more affordable than sable, yet they have a similar, soft feel. They're made of a blend of ox hair and synthetic fiber, and they're dyed to resemble red sable. They're used for oils and acrylics.

Synthetic brushes are available in several different compositions, including nylon. Some are designed with little pockets in the filaments and some with bumps in the bristles to hold the paint. Those that are dyed a gold color have the feel of sable; the white ones feel more like bristle. For the most part, synthetic brushes are durable and cost efficient.

Having a brush with the right shape for the job is every bit as important as having the right quality. Most of the brushes used for the projects in this book are flats, rounds, fans, flat rounds, or liners. In several projects, some of these brushes are modified to perform a specific task better. Play with all of the different brush shapes to discover their natural strokes, capabilities, and tricks. Try using the flat brush to create squares and diamonds, to elongate the end of a diamond, to make a loosely shaped triangle by positioning and sweeping one end of the flat. Rounds can be used to make the necessary shapes for painting folk art and for creating petals, leaves, and commas with a single brush stroke. A little experimenting with a paint-filled brush, a blank piece of paper, and pressure variations will reveal a multitude of shapes to you.

Some examples of flat brushes are shown on the next page. A flat brush has square-cut bristles, which are usually synthetic, and although not an expensive brush, it's versatile and performs well. The flat artist's brushes shown in the photograph have a mixture of synthetic and red sable bristles and are used to apply oil-based paint where a fine smooth surface is desired. The three larger flat brushes at the lower left have a variety of uses. The brush on the left is made of hog bristle and is used to blend or drag paint and to apply a smooth coat of paint to a large surface. I save this brush for oil-based paints. The brush in the middle is a sable blend that is used for applying a smooth coat of paint on smaller projects. It's also used for applying polyurethane. The brush to the right is a polyester brush with velvetized tips that I use for applying primer on rougher surfaces. I also use this brush to remove sawdust and other debris from corners and tight spots.

A brush round actually has a tapered tip that comes to a fine point. The finer the point, the better the brush. Use the round brush for detail work or small areas where a fine point will come in handy.

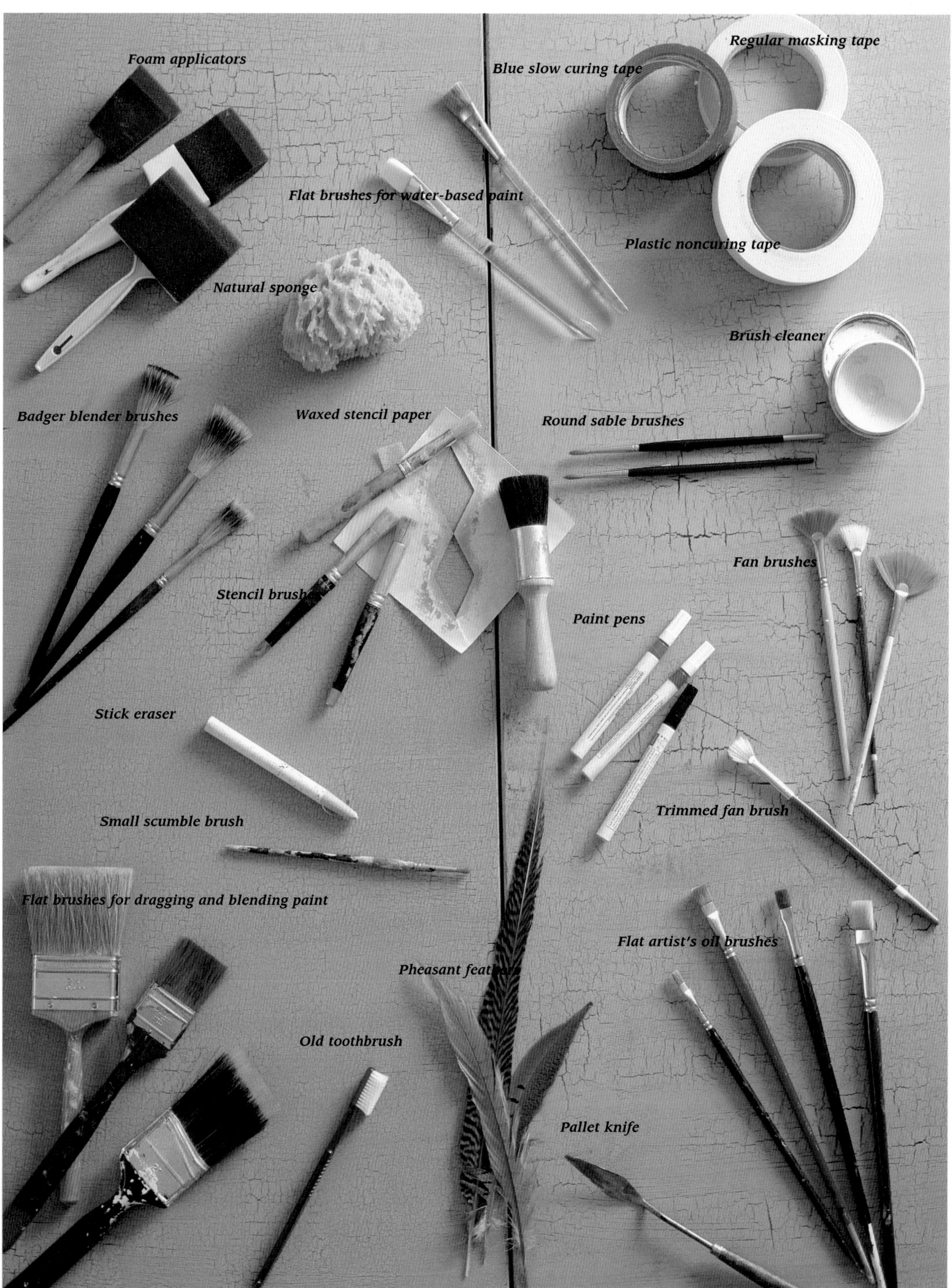
Foam applicators
Blue slow curing tape
Regular masking tape
Flat brushes for water-based paint
Plastic noncuring tape
Natural sponge
Brush cleaner
Badger blender brushes
Waxed stencil paper
Round sable brushes
Fan brushes
Stencil brush
Paint pens
Stick eraser
Small scumble brush
Trimmed fan brush
Flat brushes for dragging and blending paint
Flat artist's oil brushes
Old toothbrush
Pallet knife

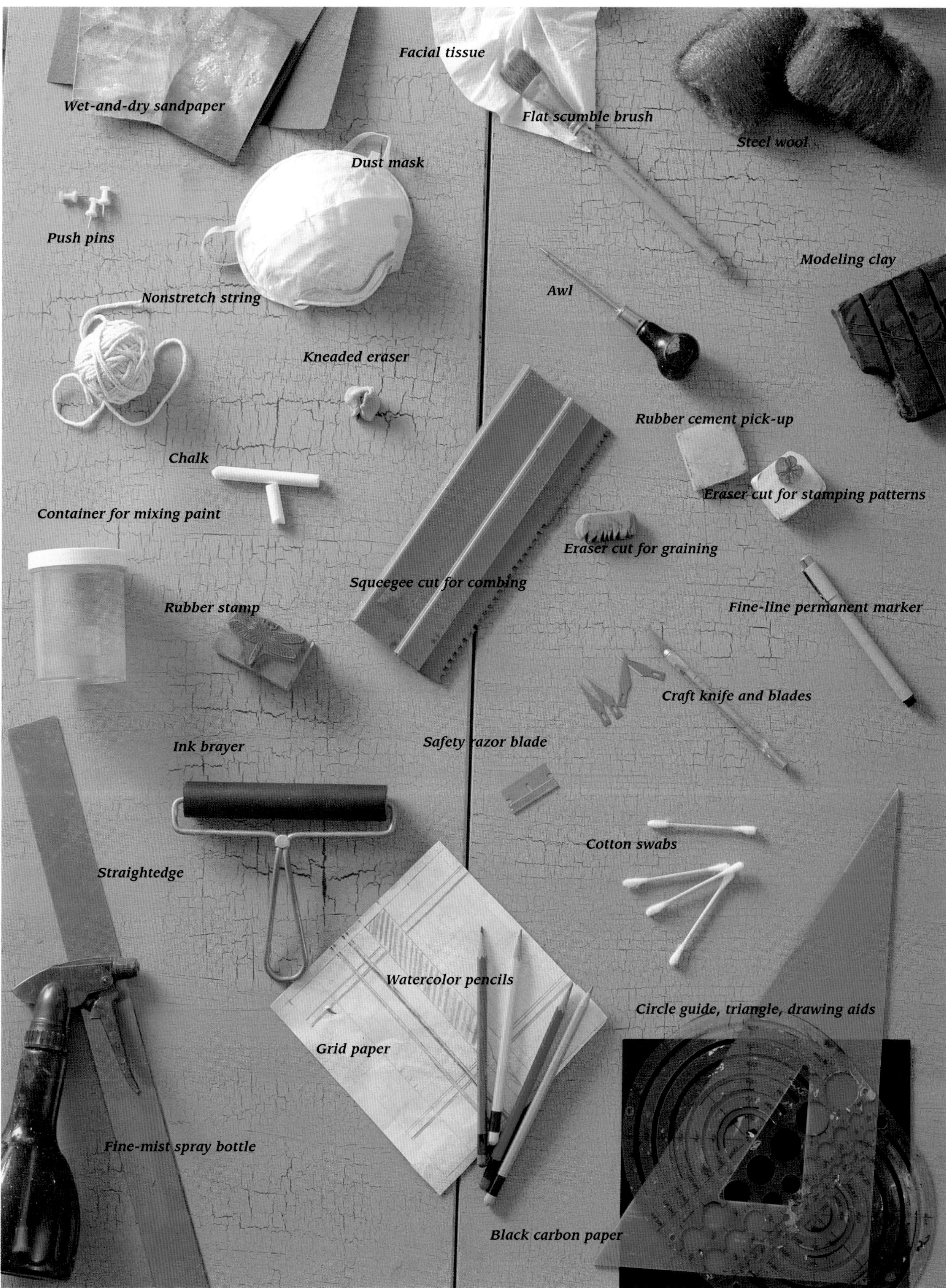
Facial tissue
Wet-and-dry sandpaper
Flat scumble brush
Steel wool
Dust mask
Push pins
Modeling clay
Awl
Nonstretch string
Kneaded eraser
Rubber cement pick-up
Chalk
Eraser cut for stamping patterns
Container for mixing paint
Eraser cut for graining
Squeegee cut for combing
Rubber stamp
Fine-line permanent marker
Craft knife and blades
Ink brayer
Safety razor blade
Cotton swabs
Straightedge
Watercolor pencils
Circle guide, triangle, drawing aids
Grid paper
Fine-mist spray bottle
Black carbon paper

Fan-shaped brushes are perfect for delicate blending and softening of color. They also make some of the best graining tools. Used dry or wet, they're well worth their price. I recommend using synthetic, gold-colored fan brushes.

Flat rounds are made from several different types of hair or bristle. For the stencil project on page 80, hog bristle or nylon will work well. The badger blender brushes are also flat rounds. They're used to soften and blend paint over larger areas than the fan brush can handle. When you blend paint with a badger brush, you use a tamping motion, which results in a different effect than the one you obtain by stroking with a fan brush or flat blender. Badger brushes come with a plastic protective sleeve. Keep the tube; it becomes an attachment tool that you can slide low over the brush hairs to give a stiffer, more easily controlled tamping blender.

The liner brush looks like an elongated round. It's used to create a continuous line without having to break for more paint. It has a very sharp point and comes in handy for detail work.

Scumble brushes are made from old artists' brushes that can no longer perform very well because their tips have been destroyed by use and abuse. To make a scumble brush, simply cut off the worn tip with a sharp safety razor blade. Place the brush flat on a cutting board, and slice through all of the bristles at once. Hold the blade almost upright (at an angle of about 85 degrees), slanting the blade end slightly toward the tip. Use scumble brushes to blend and daub your paint. Their shorter bristles are also efficient for removing stripes of paint or glaze, as in the painted inlay on pages 134–35.

Foam applicators may not be paintbrushes and may not be any good with oil-based paints, wood stains, shellac, or any polyurethane that has a base of mineral spirits, but they're inexpensive. If cleaning becomes a problem, you can afford to throw them away, and the better quality, finely grained foam applicators apply a smooth, even coat of paint when used properly.

Combing and Graining Tools

Paint can be combed or grained with any number of objects, but some tools are especially efficient for this job. One is a squeegee, which can be cut with a razor blade or craft knife to form teeth in the rubber blade. A cut squeegee was used to create the deep texture on the lid of the blanket chest on page 98.

In addition to making your own, there are combing tools available commercially. A three-sided comb makes a finer pattern than the squeegee, and each side has a different weight and texture. There are also tools that imitate actual wood grain. The grain pattern is cut in relief into rubber that is laminated to a roller or half-roller. The rubber surface is rolled a little, dragged a bit, and rolled again in the wet paint, resulting in a pattern that simulates actual wood grain. With a little practice, even an amateur can successfully produce a variety of effects.

Sponges

Natural and synthetic sponges are irreplaceable tools for anyone who wants to paint furniture. They're used to apply, remove, and clean up paint.

Natural sponges, though more expensive, are best for making patterns while applying and removing paint. The patterns of a natural sponge vary with each slight turn, giving freshness and spontaneity to your work. With water-based paint, natural sponges clean up easily and last a long time. You can rinse out oil paint by dipping your sponge into paint thinner, but this is hard on the sponge and shortens its life.

Synthetic sponges cost much less and are true workhorses. Because they cost so little, you can freely cut, dip, tear, and scrub at will with them in any medium, including oil-based paint, and then toss the spent tool into the trash. Some manmade sponges disintegrate in oil paints, however, so test your sponge first to prevent small pieces of sponge from ruining your work.

Markers, Paint Pens, and Watercolor Pencils

Markers, paint pens, and watercolor pencils are tools that you may not think of when you consider painting a piece of furniture, but they can greatly expand your repertoire of methods and effects. They're also sometimes easier for the nonprofessional to control. The unexpected can occur, however, if you combine these tools with the wrong paints and varnishes.

Markers allow you to draw lines with greater accuracy than you can obtain with a paintbrush, and they're perfect for

Watercolor pencils are easier to control than paintbrushes, and they give a crisp, tailored look to bold geometric patterns.

outlining painted areas. Keep in mind, though, that permanent markers quickly dissolve when touched with turpentine, oil paint, alcohol, and polyurethane that has a base of mineral spirits. Water-based markers have the opposite problem and must be used with oil-based products.

Paint pens are just as helpful as markers when it comes to drawing a line, ruled or freehand, but the pens don't last as long as the markers. They're also prone to leaving sudden, large blobs of paint on your work and almost as quickly drying out. If you use a paint pen, it's best to finish all of your work in a few days at most because they often don't last much longer than that once they've been opened. Be sure to cap them tightly between uses. Like permanent markers, paint pens are dissolved by oil-based products. Where they come in contact with other media, use water-based paints and stains, and seal them with a water-based polyurethane.

Watercolor pencils are, obviously, water-based, and they can even be smeared with the perspiration from your hands. It's best to "fix" the pencil marks with a light but solid coat of spray fixative, which is available at art supply stores. Follow the manufacturer's directions when you use a matte fixative, and spray outdoors if possible. For an example of a project using watercolor pencils, see page 104.

Masking Tape

The projects in this book call for three different types of masking tape. Each is distinguished by the rate at which its adhesive cures. On one type, it doesn't cure at all. No matter which kind you use, make sure that the paint won't seep under the masking tape by painting over the edge of the tape with the base color or with varnish.

Common (beige) masking tape has the shortest curing time of the three and should be left in position for eight hours at most. If you leave it any longer, it may be difficult to remove. When the tape comes off, it may leave a sticky residue that can be removed only with solvent. Use of a solvent may in turn damage water-based paints or markers used on your project.

A slower curing masking tape designed to remain in place for three to four days is available in the paint department of most home supply stores. It's colored a bright blue and can't be confused with conventional high-tack tape. It takes a little more time to burnish it into position and make sure that all of the edges are securely down.

Noncuring plastic masking tape is available at marine hardware stores. It's designed to use on boats, where it can be exposed to the hot sun indefinitely and still be removed without mishap. It's perfect over delicately painted surfaces and for masking work that will take some time to finish. You can leave it in place long enough for your water-based paints to dry and harden, and when you remove the tape, the paint doesn't come up with the adhesive.

Paints

Choosing paint can sometimes be very confusing. The major decision is the choice between water-based or oil-based paints. Water-based paint is safer, healthier, and better for the environment. It dries fast, comes in any color, goes on as smoothly as silk, and cleans up with soap and water. Why not use it for all applications? The most important reason is that it doesn't form a hard, durable surface. Polyurethane doesn't do much to help. It only places a tough barrier over a soft surface. Scratches aren't a problem, but dents are. The more coats of water-based paint there are under the varnish, the greater the possible depth of a dent.

There seems to be a direct relationship between the length of drying time and the durability of the finish. I'm sure that this can't be true for all modern polymers, but in general, oil-based paint forms a harder, stronger barrier than water-based paint. If you're working on a project where wear isn't a factor, then the scales tip in favor of the water-based medium.

It's not just durability that often makes oil-based paint the right choice for the job. With oil, you get time to work with a glaze or surface texture until it's exactly right. You have time to blend your graining, and as a direct result, you have better, softer blending. Oil-based paint glides on more luxuriously than acrylic, and its tough, matte finish is better suited for combing techniques. Matte acrylic paint won't wipe clean with a combing tool or hold up to the tool's repeated strokes. Other reasons for choosing oil-based paint are mentioned in the descriptions of specific projects. You do have a choice, though, and there are often ways to avoid the need to work with oils.

Even with all of its shortcomings—odor, more difficult clean-up, possible environmental and health hazard—using oil-based paint is similar to using an old, wooden cutting board instead of a plastic, high-tech surface. There's an indefinable, soul-satisfying pleasure that is hiding in the wooden board and in the new tube of rich, strong, saturated oil color. And I'm not convinced that the end results aren't better in oil. This isn't the Renaissance, however, and I've made an effort to use acrylic water-based paint whenever possible in the projects that follow.

Varnishes

The most commonly available varnish and the one most often used for the projects in this book is polyurethane. There are two "kinds" of polyurethane: one is thinned with mineral spirits (solvent-based) and the other with water. Both dry to a clear, tough, protective finish. Both are available glossy (the toughest), semigloss, and satin/matte. Unlike most other varnishes, water-based polyurethane doesn't yellow. Yellowing is caused by the presence of linseed oil, which *is* found in solvent-based polyurethane. Use solvent-based polyurethane over darker projects, and choose water-based polyurethane over light-colored projects unless the yellow cast is desirable.

When you're applying more than one coat, thin the polyurethane a little for the first layer. Apply polyurethane with a soft, good quality brush that you use exclusively for varnishing. Sand lightly to remove surface dirt and blemishes using wet/dry sandpaper and a little soapy water. Be careful not to sand through to the underlying layer of paint or varnish.

SPONGE PAINTING ROCKERS

Genteel rocking on the front porch has long been a custom in the southern United States. In this part of the world, rocker-sitting is practically an art form, and a line of rockers on the front porch is a good indicator of the number of adults in residence. It seems reasonable, then, that these census-taking homes for derrières should be attractive and visually exciting.

Whether lined up on the porch or arranged on the lawn, a riot of floral color splashed across these rockers might just get things rolling. Paint is the quickest and least expensive way to fill our lives with color, and no color application is easier than sponge painting. The most difficult and time-consuming element is applying the base color! The only goal to aim for in the mastery of the sponging technique is evenness and a little variety in the pattern of the imprint.

These rockers are painted in vibrant, tropical colors and are sponged in selective areas to give a textural contrast with the solid surfaces. (An added benefit of this design decision and type of application is that you can avoid areas that are difficult to reach and, therefore, sponge evenly.) The seats of the rockers have a little contrasting color woven through the slats to add visual interest.

Sponge painting can be used on any number of projects and in so many variations that the combinations are endless. You can play with subtle, sumptuous blends of color for a picture frame or mat. Perhaps a set of wooden or metal canisters could use a new face. Is the front door of your home an unbroken surface of color that is too overpowering for the rest of the house? Sponge it! Two other, more muted colors added to the strong base hue will give the door a richer, deeper surface and can tie in some of the other exterior colors. It takes only moments to master this technique, yet it's one that you can use over and over again and, if you don't want it to, it will never look the same way twice.

Materials

- Rocking chairs or any other project
- Bleach (optional)
- Household cleanser (optional)
- Exterior oil-based wood primer
- Exterior latex paint in the colors of your choice (see **Note**, page 19)
- Satin polyurethane

Tools

- #60 garnet sandpaper (optional)
- #120 garnet sandpaper
- 3" (7.6 cm) flat brush
- #320 wet/dry sandpaper
- Natural sponge that fills but fits comfortably in your palm
- Bucket of water
- Rubber or plastic gloves (optional)
- 1" (2.5 cm) flat brush
- Small rag

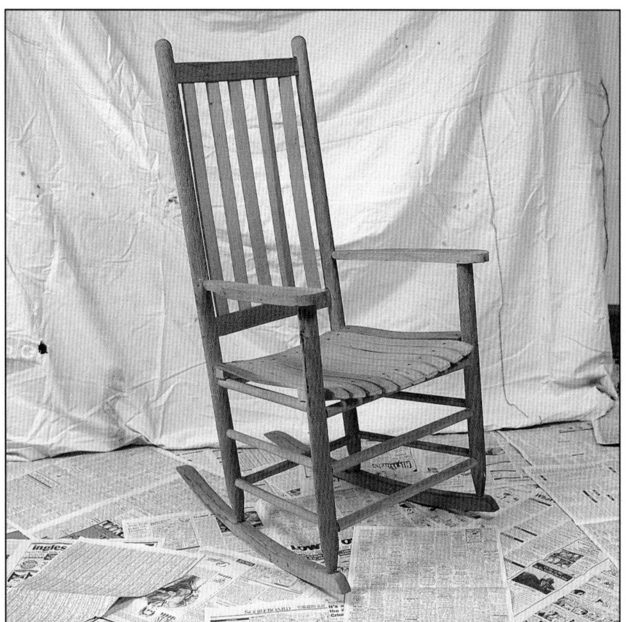

Instructions

1. These rockers were in fairly rough condition when they were purchased, and if you're working with used furniture, you may have the same dilemma. They had been allowed to weather and had mold and mildew stains all over them. Weathering isn't a problem, but mold and mildew, if not removed, will eventually destroy the new paint. Scrub them off with a 10 percent bleach solution that includes some household cleanser. Then rinse your project thoroughly with water, and allow it to dry in the sun.

2. If you're working with weathered wood, rough sand it with #60, then with #120 garnet paper before priming. With wood that is in pretty good condition, sanding with #120 paper should be sufficient.

3. I used an oil-based primer to give a hard surface that would face up to a lot of wear. To save time and avoid having to apply a base color over the primer, tint the primer. A lot of color tint was added to the primer to obtain the intensity of color that I desired. The color of the paint was

checked several times, and more tint was added until there was no room left in the can!

4. Apply the primer with the 3-inch (7.6 cm) brush. Dip the brush into the paint so that only one-third of the length of the bristles is immersed, and keep the paint away from the heel. Then tap one side of the brush against the side of the can to get rid of the dripping excess. Brush the paint onto the rocker in the direction of the wood grain. When your brush starts to run out of paint, check for drips, and return to the can for another load of paint. Check for drips, and stir your paint often. First paint the areas that are difficult to reach; then paint the rest of the project from the top down.

5. Allow the base color to dry for five days or more. Then sand the surface lightly with #320 paper and a little soapy water.

Before you begin to sponge paint, take a long look at your project. Decide just which areas you wish to sponge and which areas are likely to give you trouble because they're too close to an area you wish to leave solid. The exterior latex paint that you're using for this project is water based but permanent once it dries. You can touch up mistakes with some of the base color, but it's so much easier if you plan ahead how to hold and place the sponge in those difficult areas. If you have a difficult combination of angles and corners, practice with a damp sponge first.

6. With the white paint well mixed, dip the sponge into the water, and wring it out. Then dip one portion of the sponge into the white paint. Holding the sponge over the water, squeeze it again to distribute the paint and get rid of any excess. (All of this, of course, is much neater if you wear rubber or plastic gloves.) Now you're ready to apply the paint. Start by testing the color on the underside of your project.

7. Lightly pat the sponge against the surface at random, but aim for evenness. If you're planning to sponge more than one color, remember to leave some room. You don't want to cover up too much of your great base color. Stand back and squint at your work occasionally to make sure that you haven't neglected one area or put too much pattern on another. Also, be sure to turn the sponge once in a while.

8. When the sponge impressions start to fade, return to the white paint for a refill, and again squeeze the excess out over the water bucket. Continue in this way until you've laid on all the white paint that you want.

9. Wash out your sponge thoroughly, and change the water in your bucket. Apply the second color following the some procedure you did for the first.

10. The seat of each chair is painted in a checked pattern using the third sponge color and a 1-inch (2.5 cm) flat brush. Only a section of the seat is checkered to keep it from overwhelming the sponge work. Before painting them, measure and mark off the checks with a pencil. This will keep confusion out of the pattern and the paint in the right squares.

11. When the rockers are dry, apply the polyurethane finish using the larger brush. Then, after allowing the polyurethane to dry thoroughly, partake of a good, old southern tradition, and come "set a spell."

Note: If you don't tint the primer, you'll need a total of three colors. The base color is usually the strongest, followed by one or two more colors that are sponged on in smaller amounts. All of these rockers have white as their second color, and to tie them together as a set, the base color of another rocker is the third color.

These close-up views of the sponged rockers clearly show the four combinations of three colors used here. When you're combining colors, test the combinations first on a piece of scrap lumber. You can use a hair dryer to speed up the drying time of your test (this is *not* recommended for an actual project). Live with your sample for a few days, placing it where you can see it often. If you still love the medley after this period of time, then proceed with confidence in the results. If you tire of your selection later, you can always paint over it or add more sponged color.

Garden Bench with a Garland of Pansies

The inspiration for this bench came from a picture of an antique, pansy-covered tile. The tile was a large, horizontal rectangle with a bouquet so beautifully painted that it has forever made me a lover of pansies. The flowers had a dewy, incandescent glow and were placed on an ivory background that was the perfect contrast to the delicate colors of the pansies and their dramatic centers. The passage of time had given the tile a crazed surface, which only deepened the beauty of the image.

The dazzling pansies on this bench were painted with a pallet more exuberant than the one used on the tile that inspired me. I had intended to glaze them to subdue their brilliant colors, but I became caught up in their undaunted spirit and decided to leave them be. Even though their character is very different from my original inspiration, I'm not disappointed at all.

The background for the pansies on this bench is related conceptually to the crazed surface of the tile. The graceful backboard was first painted a rich grape color. This was covered first by a crackle glaze, then by a layer of gray-green paint. The crackle and color combination make an attractive backdrop when viewed from a distance, and when seen at close range, they reveal more interesting detail. To help the darker flower petals maintain their outline against the background, the crackle surface was sponged with a very thin wash of white paint.

The technique for doing a crackle finish is described in detail on pages 95–96, but this project is much more direct and doesn't require any of the testing. If you follow the manufacturer's directions, you'll find the application easy and trouble-free. Sponging is covered on pages 18–19.

The solid cypress bench shown here was purchased unfinished from a manufacturer in Washington, Louisiana. If you don't have a bench to paint, the pattern would complement the backboard on a dining server, the headboard of a bed, or the cornice above some window sheers.

Materials

- Bench or other project
- Primer of your choice (see page 10)
- Interior/exterior acrylic satin enamel paints: Napa purple, bluegrass green, permanent magenta, deep sage green
- Masking tape
- Crackle glaze medium
- Acrylic craft paints: bright yellow, yellow, gold, orange, red, pink, magenta, violet, purple, lavender, blue, ice blue, kelly green, leaf green, forest green, black, white
- Pattern enlarged to size
- Gesso
- Bucket of water
- Semigloss polyurethane

Tools

- 2" (5.1 cm) foam applicator
- #320 wet/dry sandpaper
- Brushes: 2" (5.1 cm) blunt end, #2, #4, and #6 artist's rounds
- Measuring cup
- Natural sponge about 3" x 4" (7.6 x 10.4 cm)
- Black carbon paper
- Ball-point pen with bright-colored ink
- Paper towels
- Pictures of pansies for reference

Instructions

1. Prepare your project for painting by priming and sanding it according to the recommendations on pages 8–10.

2. The color combination for this bench was decided after experimenting with a number of paint chips. I wanted a dramatic color medley, but these colors may not fit your decor. The best way to select your own color trio is to test their harmony by painting patches of the colors on a scrap board, butting each color against the other. The relative size of the paint patches should approximate the proportion of each color to be used on the bench. Live with this test for a few days, adjusting one or more colors if you need to, until you select a harmonious group. The following directions are written with the purple, green, and magenta in mind.

3. Using the 2-inch (5.1 cm) foam applicator or the 2-inch (5.1 cm) brush, paint the bench back and rolling arm with the Napa purple paint, and apply the green paint to the seat, sides, and legs. The foam applicator is easier in this type of situation, where you have two colors coming together at a 90-degree angle. Depending on the degree of opacity of your paint, you may need two to three coats for good coverage. Between coats, sand the dry paint with the #320 paper and a little soapy water.

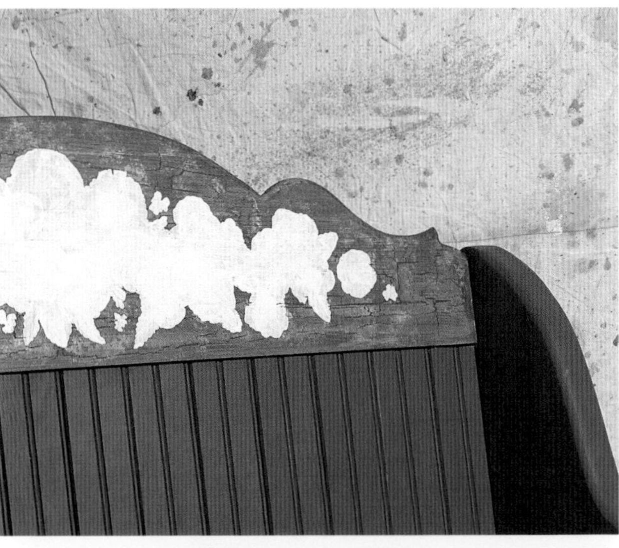

4. When the paint is dry and cured, mask the back and seat; then paint the magenta band.

5. Lay the bench flat on its back, and apply a coat of crackle medium, following the manufacturer's directions and the tips on page 92.

6. When the medium has dried for about an hour (the amount of drying time depends on the humidity in your work area), apply a coat of the deep sage green. Take care not to paint over your initial strokes. The reaction between the medium and the paint over it makes the crackle finish.

7. Allow the cracked paint to dry before mixing 1/8 cup (29.6 ml) of white paint with 1/4 cup (59.1 ml) of water. When the two are completely blended, wet and wring out your sponge, and dip it into the paint wash. Wring out the sponge, and dab it onto the upper panel on the back of the bench, overlapping the sponge pattern to cover and give texture to the muted green paint.

8. After your sponge work has dried, position the sized pattern on the panel. Measure to establish the center point, and check to make sure the pattern is perfectly horizontal. Tape the pattern down only at the top so that the masking tape can function as a hinge to flip the pattern back and forth. Slide the carbon paper underneath the pattern, carbon side down, and trace only the outline of the pattern onto the panel. Then flip the pattern back out of the way, and paint the entire pattern area with gesso, using the 1-inch (2.5 cm) brush. Allow the gesso to dry thoroughly.

9. Now flip the pattern and carbon back into position, and trace the details onto the white ground. Don't remove the pattern until you're sure that you've traced everything.

10. When you finish tracing all of the details, assemble your entire selection of craft paints, your round brush collection, a small bucket or container of water in which to clean your brushes, and some paper towels. Start painting the pansies from the center outward. Alternate from a pansy on one side of the center to one on the other as you work, balancing the color distribution as much as possible. In other words, paint one purple posy on the panel to the right of center; then pick a corresponding petal or two on the left, approximately the same distance from the center, and paint it the same color. The close but not perfect symmetry will produce a pleasing balance.

11. To render an individual flower in a simplified manner, paint the entire flower with a somewhat translucent base color such as yellow or red, which, when applied thin enough, will allow your pencil lines to show through the pigment.

12. Following the pattern lines, apply a second tone over the dry base color from the middle zone to the center of the flower.

13. Apply the third layer of paint near the center of the bloom, over the first two lighter tints.

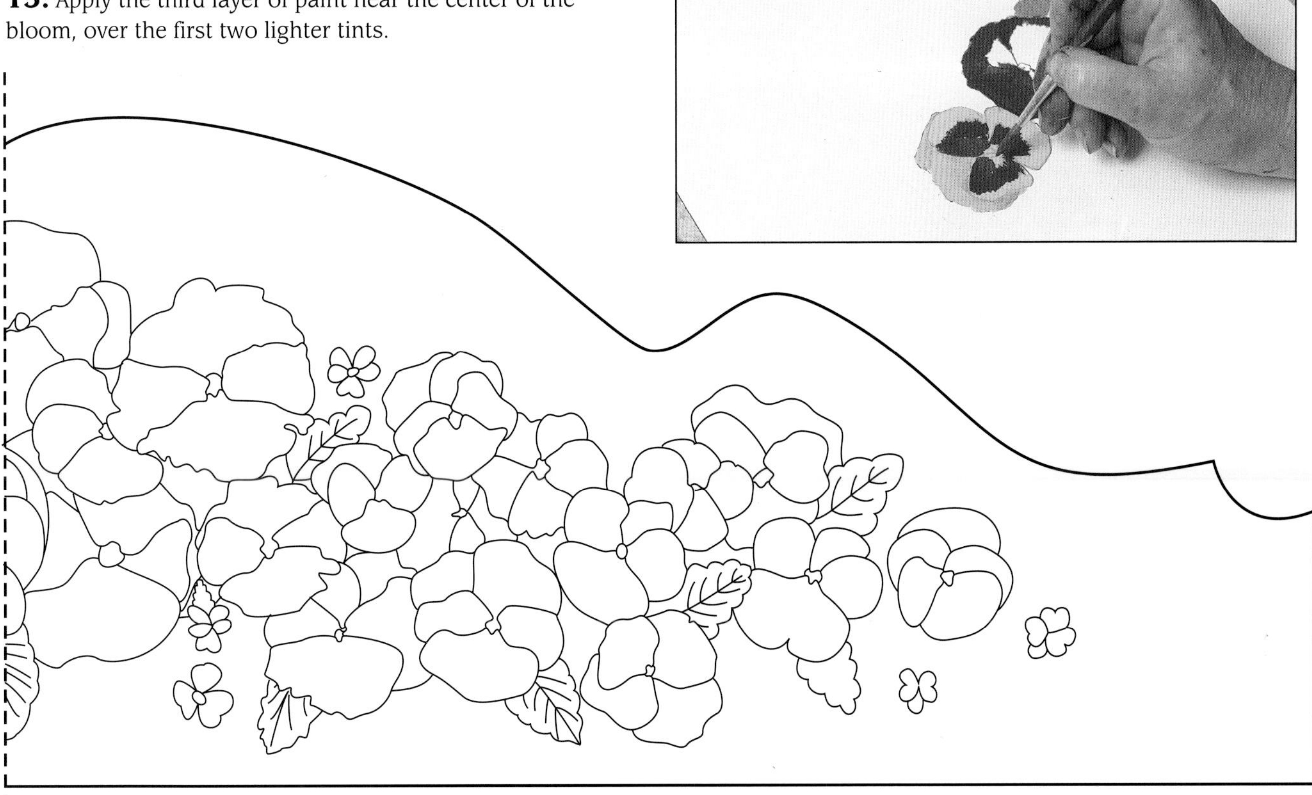

14. With a tiny dab of light leaf green at the center of the blossom to highlight the yellow pestle, your first flower is complete. Don't worry about leaving an uneven white space at the edge of the petals. The next blossom will meet your pencil line, and the white space will act as a highlight that breaks and reappears naturally along the edge of these petals. Finish painting all of the flowers in this manner, taking your time, and enjoying each pansy. To determine natural color combinations, consult flower and seed catalogues for pictures of pansies, and refer to the picture of the finished bench.

15. Paint the leaves next. Paint the whole leaf with the kelly green, applying a layer of paint thin enough to be translucent. Rinse the brush, and add the veining with the leaf green paint. When the vein dries, paint off to one side of it with the very end of the brush tip and the dark forest green. Use the forest green to make a shadow where the leaf goes under the petal of the pansy. Make this shadow in several steps. First outline the edge of the petal with the brush tip. Then dip the brush in water, blot it onto the paper towel to absorb some of the water, and make another, slightly fainter line right next to the first. Repeat this process until the line becomes fainter and fainter, and finally disappears into the leaf. Highlight the texture of the leaves by dabbing some watered-down leaf green paint in the center spaces between the veins. Then, with the full-strength leaf green paint, highlight small sections along the top edges of the leaves using the tip of your brush.

16. Allow the paint from your last inspired stroke to dry and cure for five days before applying two coats of polyurethane to the entire bench and two more to the seat area. Follow the manufacturer's directions when applying the finish layers.

Refinishing a Watch Maker's Bench

It's a lucky man who owns this watchmaker's bench that's been recycled for tying flies. The glow of the refinished oak lends warmth and charm to the bench's surroundings. This hobby work is left on display in the family room, where it makes an interesting presentation and a good conversation starter. With its attractively refinished, useful cabinet, it definitely adds to the room's atmosphere.

Hobbies are so much a part of our daily lives, and yet we don't often have time to enjoy them when all the materials are tucked away in some dank hole in the basement. I see no reason, with a few accommodations, why a person can't have an easel or collection of beads or whatever displayed right in the family room. Hobbies are great stress reducers, and they're stimulating to look at, too.

But where will you ever find such a wonderful old bench in which to store and display everything? You've probably walked right past several likely candidates in secondhand shops or antique stores. You can see in the pictures that follow just how hopeless this distressed piece of furniture looked when it was purchased.

The magic touch of Liz and Pete Sullivan transformed this discarded piece into a rich feast for the eyes. To assure our success in the similar transformation of our own projects, they share their secrets with us in the following instructions.

Materials

- Project to be refinished
- Paint and varnish remover
- White wood glue
- 6d finishing nails, as needed
- Wood filler in a medium tint
- Provincial stain
- Orange shellac
- Denatured alcohol
- Satin finish polyurethane
- Paint thinner

Tools

- Tarpaulin
- Rubber gloves
- Steel wool: #0, #1, #2, #3
- Rags
- 2 - 2" (5.1 cm) flat brushes
- Clamps
- Hammer
- Nail set
- Spackling knife
- #120 and #180 garnet sandpaper
- Clean, lint-free rag
- Vacuum cleaner
- Clean containers for mixing
- 2" (5.1 cm) flat shellac brush

Instructions

1. First remove any pieces from your project that are broken and need repair, and store them where you'll be able to find them. Stripping a piece of furniture is a messy process, so work outdoors or in an area where mess doesn't matter, and use a tarp to protect the working surface.

Start by assembling all of your tools and materials. To remove the old varnish and shellac from your piece of furniture, you'll need rubber gloves, the flat brush *not* used for shellac, paint and varnish remover, rags, and the #3 steel wool. Be sure to read and follow all of the directions and cautions that are printed on the can of remover before beginning your work.

2. With your hands protected by rubber gloves, apply the stripper (see page 9 for more details) to one side of the cabinet. Allow the stripper to sit until it eats through the old varnish; then clean off the stripper with the rags and steel wool. Repeat this process until your project is completely stripped of the old varnish.

3. At this stage, with all of the old finish gone, you're ready to proceed with any necessary repairs. Use white wood glue and clamps for this. After you've placed glue on the broken pieces of wood and returned them to their original positions, clamp them and leave them to dry undisturbed for several hours or overnight. Prevent the clamps from becoming a permanent part of your project by wiping off any excess glue with a damp rag before the glue dries.

4. This watchmaker's bench had one loose side. To repair it, Liz and Pete used 6d finishing nails, hammered and set in place.

After tacking and setting any nails that you may have needed, use your spackling knife to fill all of the holes with wood putty. Following the manufacturer's directions, allow the wood filler to dry, and refill the holes "proud." When the second application of wood filler has dried, sand the wood filler with #180 garnet paper. Remove any residue by wiping down the entire piece of furniture and vacuuming the surface.

5. Using a lint-free rag, rub the provincial stain onto all of the wood surfaces of your project. This will even out the color of the wood. Let the stain dry overnight.

6. Before proceeding, vacuum the project and the area again. Then mix two parts shellac with one part denatured alcohol in a clean container. Apply this mixture to the cabinet with the shellac brush, and allow it to dry for two hours.

7. When the shellac is completely dry, rub down all of the surfaces with #0 steel wool. Wipe the cabinet clean, and vacuum it again.

8. Using a clean container, mix four parts of polyurethane together with one part of paint thinner. Be sure to stir the polyurethane well before adding it. Then apply this mixture to your piece of furniture with a clean, 2-inch (5.1 cm) flat brush. Allow the varnish to dry overnight. Apply a second coat of polyurethane in the same manner.

9. To complete your project, clean and sand the inside of the drawers; then apply shellac.

Heart-Shaped Box with a Translucent Glaze and Painted Floral Wreath

In our home we have a place for guests to stay that we call the "sweetheart room" because it was stenciled with hearts when we bought the house. There is also a heart-shaped wreath on the door. The quilt in progress in the background of the picture on the opposite page will eventually be used in the sweetheart room. It's covered with French knots that form all kinds of hearts.

The room is an inviting place for guests to stay and for me to sit in front of the fireplace, stitching the hours away. This heart box makes a fine end table, and it holds all of my sewing paraphernalia, keeping me organized. The box is also an attractive focal point for the room.

This heart box is painted with glazes—translucent color films made by thinning paint. The glaze used for the sides and top of this project is a commercially available stain called winter white. The flowers are also painted using color glazes, but since those glazes are made by thinning acrylic craft paints with water, they're called washes.

Wooden boxes similar to the one used in this project are available from craft shops, unfinished furniture stores, and mail-order catalogues. If you wish to duplicate this project, then it won't be difficult to locate the box.

The wreath pattern would also adapt well to the headboard of a twin bed, particularly one that has been glazed first. Table tops, drawer fronts, closet doors, and blanket chests are other projects to consider for the use of this pattern and glazing technique.

Materials

- Wooden box or other project
- Winter white oil-based wood stain
- Water-based matte polyurethane
- Pattern enlarged to fit your project
- Carbon paper
- Acrylic craft paints: bright yellow, yellow, tangerine, ultra blue, crimson, leaf green, Seminole, burnt umber, white, black

Tools

- Several clean, lint-free rags
- 2" (5.1 cm) foam applicator
- #400 wet/dry sandpaper
- Ball-point pen with bright-colored ink
- 2 fine- and 1 medium-tipped black paint pens or permanent markers
- Small plastic spoon
- Small container
- #4 round artist's brush

Instructions

1. Commercially available pastel wood stains are easy to work with, and success will result if you follow the manufacturer's directions. There are just a few important points to remember. First, these glazes/stains are nearly transparent. Whatever flaws or discolorations that you see in the wood before you stain, you will also see afterward. They may be even more obvious, so prepare your piece well. Second, work in small areas. You have only one minute after applying it to wipe off the excess stain. If you put stain over too great an area, you won't be able to wipe off as much as you may have wanted. Third, stir the stain well and often. If you don't, you may end up with uneven coverage. Fourth, to avoid getting dirt in the finish, use a lint-free cloth for application of the stain and removal of the excess. Last, wipe in the direction of the grain. I applied two coats on this box and allowed it to dry four hours between coats.

2. One of the drawbacks of commercially available stains and glazes, aside from their price, is the variety of colors available. If you wish to save money and create a custom color, the following formula will prove useful. To make the glaze base, mix together one part turpentine, one part Liquin, and one part cobalt drier. (Liquin and cobalt drier are available at art supply stores.) Add the color by mixing a

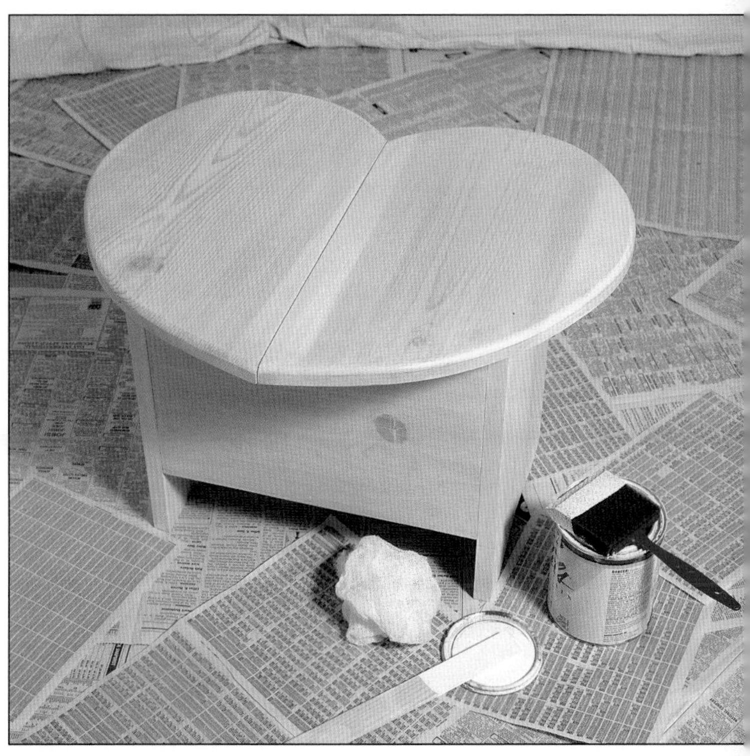

translucent artist's oil color with a small dot of white oil paint. Use a pallet knife to do your mixing. Then thin the mixture with turpentine folded in one drop at a time. When the paint is mixed well and is thinned to the consistency of milk, add it, a small amount at a time, to the base mixture. Test the color and intensity of the glaze on a piece of scrap lumber while you're mixing and adding color. The disadvantage of this homemade glaze is that it will take quite a bit longer to dry than will the commercial stain. It should be applied with a soft brush.

3. After the stain or glaze has dried, apply two coats of polyurethane. (At least 48 hours are required for the commercial stain to dry, and one week is needed for the glaze. Don't give in to temptation by applying the varnish sooner because you'll be mixing an oil-based material with a water-based finish; unless the undercoat is fully cured, the two materials won't make a good bond.) Allow sufficient drying time between coats of polyurethane.

4. When the polyurethane is dry, sand it very lightly with soapy water and #400 paper. See page 8 for details.

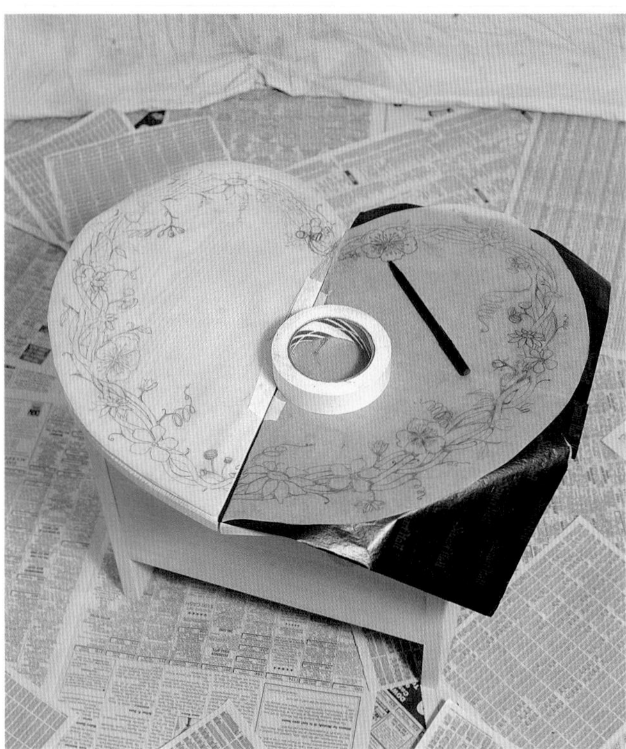

5. Tape the sized pattern securely to the lid of the box so that it's hinged with tape along one side of the pattern. Insert carbon paper between the pattern and the box, making sure that you have the carbon side down. Trace the pattern using the ball-point pen, and don't remove the tape from the pattern until you're sure that you've traced the complete wreath.

6. Using the medium-point paint pen, outline the grapevine portion of the wreath, excluding the delicate tendrils.

7. In a small container (I use old jar lids), mix one spoonful of ultra blue paint with a very small amount of white and plenty of water to make a wash. Using the #4 artist's brush, play with the wash on a piece of paper. Dip the tip of your

brush into some water to make the wash thinner, or add more pigment to make the color stronger. Start painting at the center of a bloom. Circle the center, making a swipe of color; then touch the tip of your brush into the water, and continue painting out to the edge of the petal. This should give you a color gradation from darker to lighter.

8. Paint all of the blue flowers, and continue with the pink ones. The pink color results from making a crimson wash.

9. The yellow flowers are painted somewhat differently. First paint the entire bloom with a wash of bright yellow. When the bright yellow dries, apply a wash of yellow at the inner edge of the petals and a tangerine wash on the tips. Wash the centers with burnt umber. Add dots of undiluted yellow paint to the center of the blue and pink flowers as well as on the ends of the stamens in the pink blossoms. Paint some of the buds with undiluted color.

10. Paint the green of the leaves and their immediate stems with the solid color rather than a wash. To give them dimension, paint some of the leaves in two shades of green. Paint the entire leaf with the lighter green; then after the first color dries, paint the lower half of the leaf with the darker shade.

11. When all of the paint is dry, sharpen the image by outlining the flowers, leaves, and vine tendrils with the fine-pointed black paint pen. If you have trouble using the paint pen, then try using a fine-line water-proof marker.

12. Once everything is dry, it's time to add two coats of water-based polyurethane.

Rag, Drag, and a Lattice-Work Pattern on a 1950s Hutch

In the 1950s, a home decorated in the Early American style often included a dining room set that looked similar to this hutch and the table and chairs shown in later chapters. This hutch and ones like it were often made of solid maple and were able to withstand all of the punishment that a family with six children had to offer. At least this one did. This stout piece of furniture has served more than one generation of my family and now has been passed on to me. My mother will be wide eyed when she sees what I've done to one of her old, sentimental favorites!

We have no need of a second dining room set in our home, so I decided to paint the cabinet to go into our shady little riverside cottage. There, a long white wall in the living area demands a bright spot of color. The original maple finish wasn't colorful enough, but now that the cabinet is as bright as a sunflower, I feel sure it will cheer all my damp, foggy mornings for years to come.

The sunflower yellow of this hutch is glazed by ragging and dragging, which mutes and softens the base color, giving it richness, subtlety, and depth. A layer of varnish between the base and the glaze prevents the glaze from staining the base color and strengthens the illusion of depth.

Ragging and dragging is an easily learned glazing technique. First a glaze is applied to the base color using a brush or cloth. A bunched rag is then pressed into the wet glaze to leave an imprint. The impressions of the cloth are subdued by dragging a dry blender brush lightly across the surface. Ragging and dragging gets a little dicey when you have converging corners, but it's less difficult than ragging and rolling. (In that process, you roll the bunched rag along each surface.) Still, for your first project, it's best to rag and drag on flat or outside surfaces.

You can use either water-based or oil-based paint for this technique. Oil-based paint allows more time for toying with the finish or removing all of the paint and starting over if necessary. When you're working on a large project, it's best to use oil paint because the glaze will dry at a fairly slow rate. For a project this small, and with the added advantage of segmented spaces, water-based paint can be used. I try to use water-based paint whenever possible; however, it's not appropriate for all applications. See page 15 for more information on paints.

Before painting the hutch, I took a long, hard look at its proportions and decided that it was cute, short, and fat. Because the cottage wall demanded a piece with a taller, leaner look, a few simple modifications and additions were necessary. A detail board was removed from the server, and the base board was trimmed flush with the sides of the cabinet. To add height and make the top of the shelf section capable of holding books, a piece of trim was added. This was all done at a local shop at minimal cost. You can compare the two photographs on page 34 to see the few changes.

The shop also sanded and prepared the old finish for painting. This included bleaching the stain out of the shelves and the top of the server with a three percent solution of hydrogen peroxide. The peroxide was brushed on and allowed to sit until the wood lightened; then it was wiped off with a damp sponge, and the wood was rinsed with clean water. After a light sanding, the wood was ready for a clear coat of polyurethane.

Materials

Wooden project
Primer of your choice (see page 10)
2 rolls 1"-wide (2.5 cm) masking tape
Acrylic latex matte enamels: yellow, off white
Acrylic craft paints: yellow, palomino, dusty mauve, medium ultra blue, rain-forest green, burnt sienna, burnt umber
Acrylic painting medium
Water-based matte polyurethane

Tools

Fine garnet sandpaper
#400 wet/dry sandpaper
2" (5.1 cm) flat brush
3" (7.6 cm) flat brush
Clean mixing container
Clean, lint-free rags
1 or 2 - 2-1/2" (6.4 cm) flat blender brushes
Long straightedge
90° triangle
Yellow watercolor pencil
1" (2.5 cm) flat brush

Instructions

1. Before priming, disassemble your piece as much as possible. On this cabinet, the shelf section was detached from the base, and the back panel of the shelf section and all of the hardware and handles were removed. The removal of the back made it much easier to paint, and the ragging and dragging could be done without angles and corners getting in the way.

2. Following the guidelines on pages 8–10, clean, prime, and sand your project.

3. Mask the shelves with tape to protect them from paint. Using the 2-inch (5.1 cm) brush, apply two or three coats of the off-white latex paint to the door and drawer fronts, shelf sides, top molding of the shelf section, base trim board at the back of the shelves, and any wooden pulls. You need a good, solid white surface, and it's better to use two or three thinned coats of latex rather than one or two thick coats. Thin the paint with a little water so that it flows on smoothly with no drag to the brush strokes. Then remove the masking tape from the shelves, and allow the white paint to dry for five days before continuing.

4. Using the yellow paint and a 2-inch (5.1 cm) brush, paint the cabinet box and back board of the shelf section. Several coats of paint may be necessary to get an even finish. Sand lightly between coats with #400 paper and a little soapy water.

5. When the paint is dry, use the 3-inch (7.6 cm) brush to apply a top coat of polyurethane. Allow this to dry for 24 hours.

6. In a clean container, combine six parts acrylic medium, one part burnt sienna, one part burnt umber, and four parts water. Mix well. Dip a clean rag into the glaze, and wipe the glaze onto the yellow painted surface one section at a time, working in small areas only.

7. Before the glaze can dry, crumple a clean cloth in the palm of your hand. Holding it firmly but loosely, lightly press the cloth into the fresh wet glaze, removing some of the glaze and leaving the impressions of the cloth. Change the crumple pattern of the cloth every now and then by rearranging it in your palm and turning a clean side out.

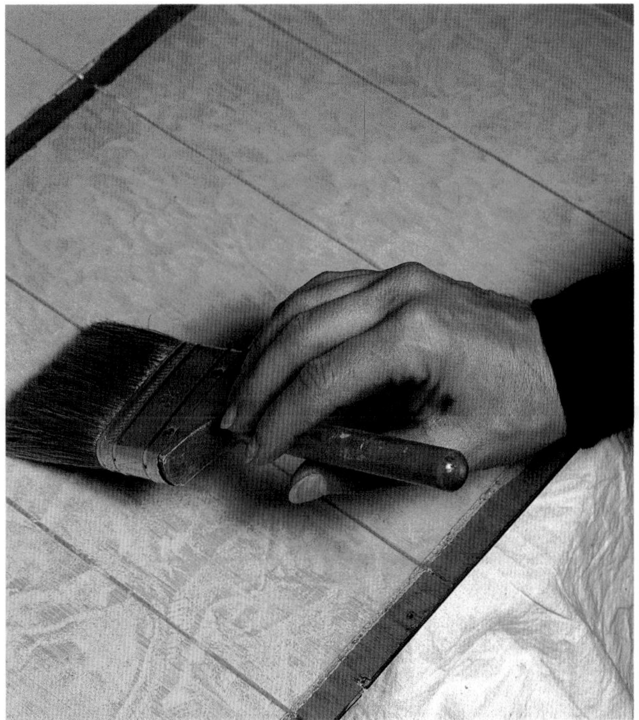

8. When you've finished ragging one glazed section and while the glaze is still wet, it's time to drag. This is done with the clean, dry blender brush. Holding the brush firmly in your hand, place the flat edge at the top of the glazed area and lightly draw it straight down to the bottom of the glaze pattern.

9. Complete all of the areas to be ragged and dragged following these steps. If one area is uneven or not right for some reason, quickly wipe the glaze off with a damp sponge, and reapply it. You can store any leftover glaze in a tightly capped container.

10. To complete the drawer and door section of the hutch, you must first reassemble all of the pieces of the cabinet with the exception of the drawer and door pulls. Once you have it all together, lay the cabinet on its back with the drawers facing up. Measure the height and width of the cabinet front to find the exact center, and mark the center with the watercolor pencil. With the watercolor pencil, draw a square the size of the area you want to have latticed on the front of the cabinet, positioning the square so that it has the same center point as the cabinet. Using the straightedge and the watercolor pencil, draw a diagonal line from corner to corner through the center point. Then draw a second diagonal line connecting the other two corners. Extend the diagonal lines beyond the square to fit a vertical or horizontal area. The lattice on this cabinet fills a horizontal rectangle.

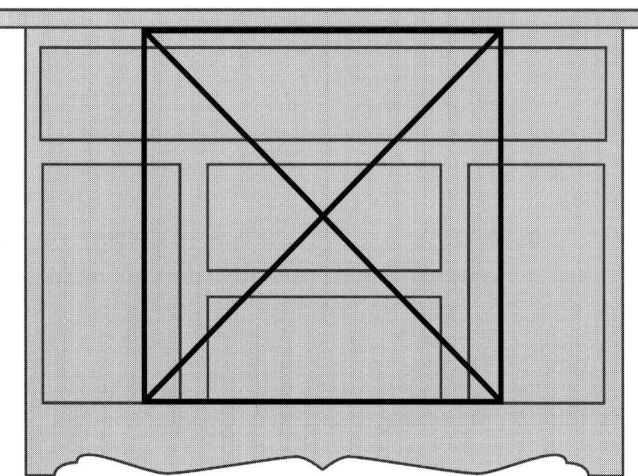

11. Begin taping for the lattice work by placing a piece of masking tape along the top side of one diagonal line. Run the tape from top to bottom, and smooth it firmly in place, making sure the edges are down. Now butt another piece of tape parallel to and at the edge of the first piece of tape, but don't smooth it down. This piece of tape is merely a spacer for the next piece of masking tape, which is placed parallel to and at the exact edge of the spacer tape. When you've positioned the piece of tape next to the spacer tape and burnished down all of its edges, remove the spacer tape, and reapply it next to the newly burnished piece of tape.

Continue in this manner using a piece of tape as a spacer between lengths of tape that are burnished into position until the drawers and door fronts are covered with a lattice of tape. If you're having trouble visualizing this, look again at the finished cabinet, and imagine that all of the white diagonal stripes are pieces of burnished masking tape and that the spaces between are where the spacer tape was.

12. It's easiest if you tape all of one diagonal first before working on the cross diagonal. Make sure that your tape goes from the top to the bottom of the cabinet in one solid piece.

13. Use more masking tape to completely cover all the yellow sections of the cabinet around the doors and drawers.

14. Before painting the different colors in the lattice pattern, the masking tape must be sealed with another coat of off-white base paint applied with the 1-inch (2.5 cm) brush. Be sure that you get the paint into the corners of the squares formed by the masking tape. This coat of paint is what will keep the color from bleeding under the masking tape.

15. Starting at the top center of your lattice, count the number of diagonal rows of squares, and divide the total by five or the number of colors you'll be using. Make marks on the masking tape to indicate where the color breaks will occur. For this hutch, it was every three rows.

16. Assemble a small bucket of water, the 1-inch (2.5 cm) brush, paper towels or rags, and all of the paint that you'll need for the color portion of the lattice work. Using a "dirty" brush, the colors are blended one into the other directly on the painted surface while the paint is still wet. Dirty in this sense means that you don't wash the brush between colors.

17. Starting at the top center of the cabinet, apply a coat of yellow to three rows of white squares. The first row has only one square. Without cleaning your brush, apply three rows of palomino paint, letting your brush be depleted as you paint. With an almost empty brush, apply more yellow over the first row of palomino to blend it. Then brush over the last row of yellow to blend in any little bit of palomino that is still on your brush.

18. Rinse your brush, and dry it quickly on a paper towel or rag. Dip your brush into the mauve, paint the next three sections of squares, and blend the mauve into the last row of palomino. Now dip your brush into the blue, and paint the next three rows. Then wash and pat dry your brush. Blend a little mauve paint into the top row of the blue. After cleaning the brush once more, paint the remaining rows green, blending the green into the last row of blue. To complete the color wheel you can blend a little yellow into your last row of green.

19. Allow the paint to dry to the touch; then remove the masking tape in the opposite order in which it was applied. You should remove the tape the same day that you applied it, or the adhesive will cure, and it will become more difficult to get it all off easily. Touch up any leaks of color that you may have had with the white paint.

20. Paint the sides of the cabinet following the same procedure as the front.

21. When all of the paint has dried and cured, reassemble the entire cabinet. Using the 2-1/2-inch (6.4 cm) brush, coat the entire cabinet twice with polyurethane. Rub the unpainted wood shelves with fine steel wool between coats of polyurethane, and apply a third coat to them.

Marbled Porphyry Column

The word porphyry comes from the Greek word for purple and refers to the reddish purple stone that was used by the Greeks and Romans to carve columns and other decorative items. The column shown here has been painted with a color variation of porphyry, which creates a totally different personality for this inexpensive terra cotta post. (It's shown in its original finish in the photograph below.) The pillar has been dressed up further with a few lines of marbling. Although the marbling gives even greater depth to the surface, porphyry is a technique that is interesting enough to stand alone.

Because it resembles ancient stone, a porphyry finish is an obvious choice for a classic column. A contemporary touch is added with the use of four wooden balls to support the plate-glass top. Slicing wedges out of the balls gives the balls more dimension and adds an excuse to vary the paint color on each ball.

One of the criteria for choosing a pillar that will be used as a table or plant stand is that it must be level and perpendicular to the ground. This is a much more important quality than having a smooth, flawless surface. Unfortunately, this pillar is more of a leaning tower. I compensated for a poor choice by adding pads of felt under two corners of the base.

Porphyry is an easy procedure to master, and it fulfills all of those urges that we have to throw paint around. As might be expected, it tends to get a little messy. Protect your work area from spatters, or work in a space where mess doesn't matter.

Materials

- Terra cotta pillar or other object
- White gesso*
- Acrylic paints for column: black, white, pink, rain-forest green, burnt sienna, old parchment
- Small plastic containers for mixing
- Paper towels
- Water-based gloss varnish
- 4 wooden balls 2" (5.1 cm) in dia. with quarter wedges cut out
- Acrylic paint for balls: white, pink, rain-forest green, ultra blue
- Epoxy glue
- 4 - 1" (2.5 cm) nails with heads snipped off
- 14" x 14" x 1/4" (35.6 cm x 35.6 cm x 6 mm) piece of plate glass

*Use acrylic white primer if you're not painting on terra cotta

Tools

- Rags
- Tack rag
- #400 sandpaper
- 1" (2.5 cm) flat brush
- Spray bottle with fine mist adjustment
- 1/4" (6 mm) bristle brush
- Old toothbrush
- Feather, about 6" (15.2 cm) long, with a sharp point
- #2 fan brush
- Natural sponge

Instructions

1. Dust off the pillar, first with a rag, then with a tack rag. Gesso is the best primer on terra cotta; it helps keep the paint from peeling off the porous surface. Apply two good coats. When the gesso is thoroughly dry, sand the finish lightly, and wipe it down with a tack cloth.

2. To make the porphyry base glaze, mix together approximately one part black paint with eight parts varnish and three parts water. Using the flat brush, paint on a coat of the dirty-looking wash, working from one section of the pillar to the next, giving special attention to the crevices and anywhere else that dirt might concentrate. This is done not to make the column look older, but to highlight its form. If the wash runs too much, dab at it with the brush or a paper towel. This dabbing may leave a texture, which is acceptable and even desirable. You may need to add more of the paint mixture to the crevasses to emphasize the form because the porphyry finish tends to disguise details.

You can choose any combination of four or five project colors that will work for your color scheme. The three turquoise eggs shown in the photograph above are examples of the textures and colors that can be created using the porphyry technique.

3. After the wash glaze has dried, add a coat of varnish. Then the real fun begins. Having predetermined your color scheme, mix your first color. Start with the color that you wish to be least dominant. If you're attempting to duplicate the pillar shown here, then mix the green with the white on a ratio of one to three.

4. Place the pillar in a horizontal position, and spritz it with very little water. Then dab on the green paint in a random pattern, making dots about 1/8 inch (3 mm) or smaller. Covering about 10 percent of the area, make lots and lots of dots of various sizes. Dots that get too big can be dabbed away with a paper towel or misted lightly to soften them. The paint should move and flow slightly with the water, creating subtle patterns.

5. As soon as the paint and water seem to have stopped flowing, it's time to turn the pillar and work on the next side. Don't be horrified by all the drip marks revealed when you turn the pillar; they will add muted depth and texture in the end. Repeat the water and dabbing procedure on this side, continue to the other two sides, and finish with the top. Then allow this coat to dry well.

6. When the pillar is completely dry, add a coat of varnish. The varnish not only protects your first layer of porphyry, but it also gives the finished piece the illusion of depth that is found in polished stone.

7. Mix the next paint color. I used one part pink, two parts white, and four parts old parchment. Repeat the steps used for the first color until all the sides and top are painted.

8. Add another coat of varnish. After this coat has dried, smooth the finish very gently with the #4/0 steel wool.

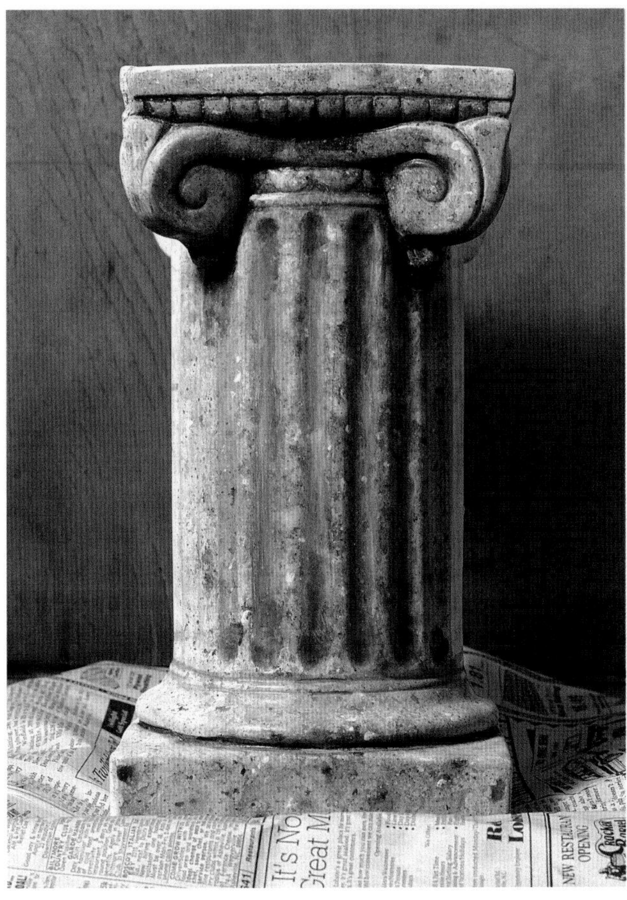

9. Mix the third color—I used straight burnt sienna—and repeat the above process.

10. The fourth color is black paint mixed with a little water to give it the consistency of ink. This is applied with the toothbrush. To practice the technique, dip the brush in a little paint, and run the tip of your finger through the brush, spattering paint onto a piece of scrap paper. Continue practicing until you can produce dots the size of fly specks with some reliability. Then apply this technique to all sides of the column. If you get any big blobs, clean them off gingerly with a damp cotton swab. When this step is complete, coat the whole surface with varnish, and allow it to dry.

11. To produce the marbling effect, mix together two drops of black paint, four drops of white, and four drops of water. This will give you a charcoal-gray paint. Dip the tip of the feather into the paint, and run it on a diagonal across the top of the column and down the side. Change direction as you go over the top edge, again as you reach the lower rim, and again on the face of the base. Go back to the beginning, and add small side veins going off at 45-degree angles from the main vein. The side veins should dwindle to nothing after about 1 or 2 inches (2.5 or 5.1 cm). Work small sections at a time, and while the paint is still wet, soften the veins by lightly dragging a fan brush over them in a sideways motion.

12. Repeat this process on the other side of the pillar, picking up the main vein from where you originally started. Once the veining has dried thoroughly, add two or more layers of gloss varnish.

13. The balls, painted with almost white shades of the same pink and green used on the pillar, add a contemporary note that keeps the classic form of the pillar from being taken too seriously. The pink and green paint, as well as the palest shade of blue on the exterior of the ball, are all mixed by adding one drop of color to a capful of white paint.

14. Sand the balls until they're smooth. After mixing the pink color, apply two coats of paint to one inside face of each ball, sanding between coats. When the paint is completely dry, place a piece of masking tape at the apex of the angle over the pink paint. This will give a sharp edge to the green paint applied to the other inside face. As soon as the green is dry, carefully remove the tape. Mix the blue paint, and apply it to the outside of the ball.

15. After the paint has dried, drill a 1/2-inch (1.3 cm) hole in the bottom of each ball. Vary the "bottom" from ball to ball so that the position of the wedge cut, when attached to the pillar top, changes from one ball to the next. Measure and mark a 1-inch (2.5 cm) distance in from the side and front of the pillar at all four corners, and drill a hole 1/2 inch (1.3 cm) deep. Mix up a little epoxy glue, place a small amount on the tip of one of the headless nails, and insert the glued end into the ball. Add epoxy to the other end of the nail, and insert it into the pillar top. When the glue is dry, you're ready to add the clean glass top and your favorite plant.

Contemporary Whimsy Animates a Child's Table and Chairs

Hannah is our youngest niece and godchild. This little cherub plays in an enchanted land by the sea that is full of fanciful animals and is called Hannah's Hona Lee. Her playroom walls are covered with painted animals, all gathered there to amuse her and keep her company. Hannah is delighted by all of her small animals, and I, being a godmom, had to design something for Hannah's Hona Lee, too.

These chummy animal chairs will engage an animal-loving child and be totally at home in a child's bedroom or play area. Well coated with high gloss polyurethane, the set of table and chairs will stand up to plenty of abuse from pencils, paints, and playful activities.

Materials

- Child-sized wooden chairs and table
- Wooden craft shapes: 2 - 1-3/4" (4.4 cm) eggs, 2 - 2" (5.1 cm) balls, 4 - 2" (5.1 cm) wheels, 4 - 1/4" x 2-1/2" (6 mm x 6.4 cm) dowels, and 1 - 1-1/2" (3.8 cm) ball cut into quarters
- Rectangle of wood approx. 2" x 1-3/8" x 1-3/8" (5.1 cm x 3.5 cm x 3.5 cm); exact size determined by width of chair leg (see below)
- Wood glue
- Primer of your choice (see page 10)
- Acrylic paints: bright pink, bright yellow, nonmetallic gold, light brown, golden brown, purple, white, black
- Patterns enlarged to fit
- Carbon paper
- Masking tape
- High-gloss polyurethane

Tools

- Saw
- Clamps
- 2" (5.1 cm) flat brush
- #240 and #320 sandpaper
- Drill with 1/4" (6 mm) bit
- Vise (optional)
- Ball-point pen with bright-colored ink
- 1/2" (1.3 cm) flat brush
- #4 round artist's brush
- Small natural sponge
- Pencil

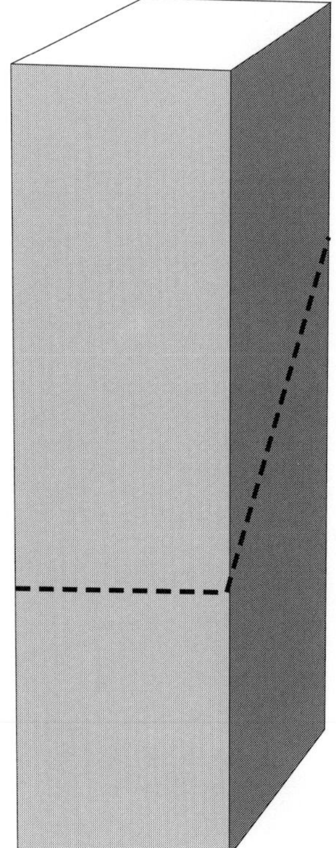

Instructions

1. Begin by preparing your pieces for assembly. Trim the ends off each quarter cut from the 1-1/2-inch (3.8 cm) ball, making a "paw" that is as wide as your chair leg. In my case, the finished width is 1-3/8 inches (3.5 cm). Take the 2-inch-long (5.1 cm) rectangle of wood that is as wide and thick as your chair leg, and cut it on a diagonal to form two wedges, each measuring 1/2 inch (1.3 cm) high at one end and 1-1/2 inch (3.8 cm) at the other. These will become the "hooves" for the other chair legs.

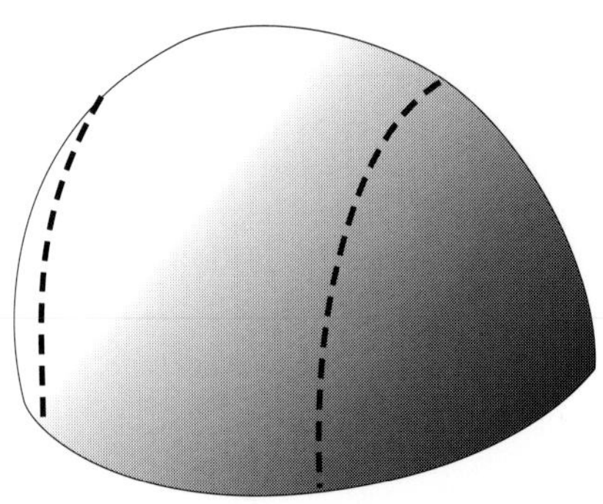

2. Glue and clamp the paws flush with the floor onto the front legs of one chair. A piece of paper placed between the floor and the legs will keep your project from attaching itself to the floor. Glue and clamp the wedge-shaped hooves in the same manner.

3. After the glue has dried, sand and prime all of the surfaces of the chairs and table.

4. At the top center of each of the supports for the chair back, drill a 1/4-inch-diameter (6 mm) hole 1 inch (2.5 cm) straight down. A piece of tape 1 inch (2.5 cm) up the shaft of the bit will help you make the hole the correct depth.

Now drill a 1/4-inch (6 mm) hole 1 inch (2.5 cm) deep into the wooden balls and the larger ends of the wooden eggs. To do this accurately, you may need to clamp the wooden shapes into a vise. If so, protect them with a damp kitchen sponge. Most likely, you will need to drill out the centers of the wooden wheels to accommodate the dowels. Check the fit on all of these pieces by assembling them in position on the chair but don't glue them together until all of the decorative painting is complete.

5. Paint the seat of the lion chair solid yellow, and leave the giraffe chair white. Before continuing on the lion chair, allow the paint to dry thoroughly.

6. Tape your sized pattern to the back of the chair seat so that the tape functions as a hinge. It may be necessary to notch the pattern to fit all the way to the back of the seat. Slide the carbon paper, carbon side down, under the pattern, and use the ball-point pen to trace the face of the giraffe (the chair with hooves) or the lion (the chair with paws) onto the seat.

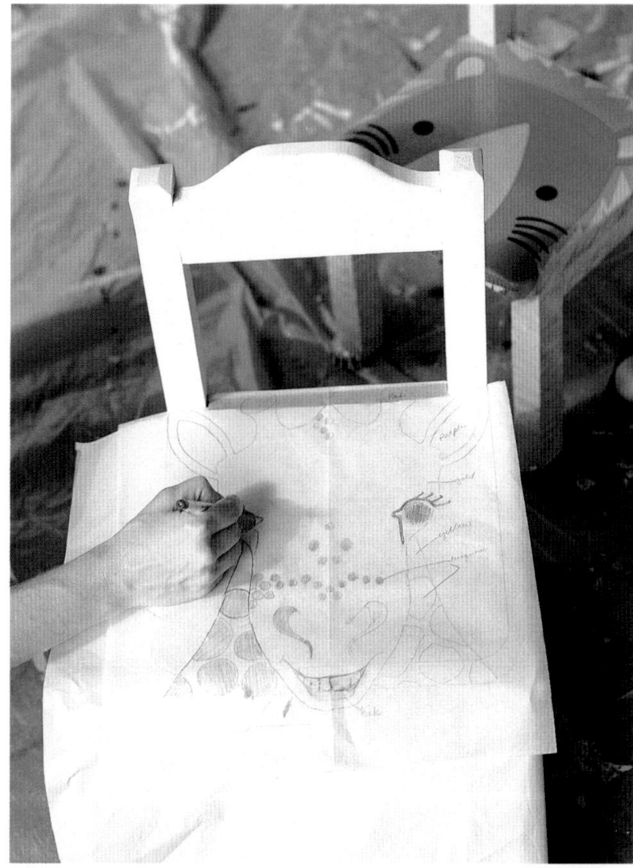

To start with, you should trace only the major shapes. For the giraffe these include the ears, horns, head, and neck. On the lion you should trace the mane, ears, ear shadow, nose, and head. Lift the pattern, and flip it back behind the seat. Don't remove the tape or the pattern, though.

7. Paint the entire head of the giraffe—ears, horns, and all—using the golden brown paint and the 1/2-inch (1.3 cm) flat brush. With the same brush, paint the neck using the bright yellow paint.

Paint the lion's mane using the gold paint and 1/2-inch (1.3 cm) brush. Then paint the head and ears using the turquoise paint and the 1/2-inch brush, leaving the nose and ear shadows the yellow base color.

8. Flip the pattern and carbon paper back into position on the giraffe, and trace all of the other facial and neck details. Paint the tongue and horn tips pink. The shadows of the ears are purple. The spots are turquoise, and the teeth are white. The eyes, nose, mouth outline, and teeth outline are all black. Use the #4 artist's brush for painting these details.

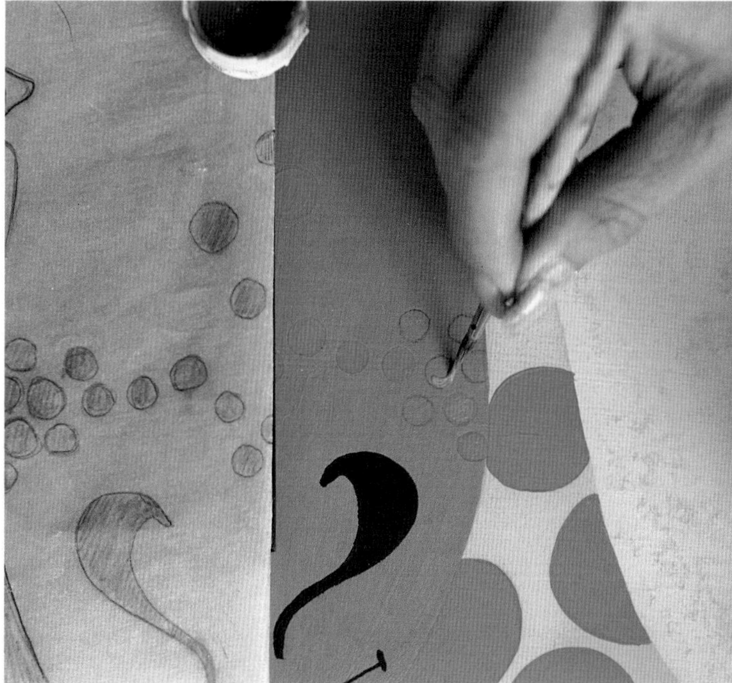

If you have trouble making a fine outline with a brush, you can use a paint pen. However, polyurethane acts as a solvent on paint pens and permanent markers, so you have to spray a fixative on them before using polyurethane. Alternatively, you can use water-based polyurethane, but it isn't as hard or durable as the type that has a mineral spirit base.

9. Trace and paint the details of the lion following the same general instructions. The lion's nose is brown, his lips pink, and teeth white. His eyes, whiskers, teeth separations, and split lip are black.

10. Sponge the background of the giraffe seat, seat supports, chair legs, and back with the yellow paint. Dilute the paint with a small amount of water so that the color will almost blend with the white primer and give the chair a sunny, cream color. If you're not familiar with sponging, the technique is explained on pages 18–19. Use a light touch with the sponge, and be careful not to come too close to the giraffe. Leave a halo of white around his head.

11. Continue the spots from the giraffe's neck down the chair legs. Using a pencil, draw irregular spots that decrease in size as you go lower on the leg, and stop them altogether about 2 inches (5.1 cm) from the foot.

12. Paint the giraffe's feet purple from the wedge down, and add a 3/4-inch (1.9 cm) strip at the base of the back legs. To complete the illusion of a hoof, paint a small, black keyhole shape on the front of each wedge.

13. The legs of the lion are done with the 1/2-inch (1.3 cm) flat brush and thinned gold paint. Lightly tamp the tips of the brush at irregular intervals along each leg, giving it a furry texture. Paint the paws solid gold, and add toenails using the #4 artist's brush and black paint. The furry texture is carried about halfway up the back supports and is repeated on the seat supports.

14. Following the same general procedure, trace the patterns, and paint the birds and monkeys onto the chair backs and wooden shapes. The bodies of the birds are purple, and the wings and tails are turquoise. The monkey bodies are also turquoise. Paint the wheel collars yellow, and add a wavy line of pink with purple dots between the waves for accent.

15. Glue the heads, dowel rods, and wheel collars together. Apply glue to the ends of the dowels, and insert them into the drilled holes in the chair backs. When the glue is dry, test to make sure that you can't pull the assembly apart.

16. The table is painted much the same way as you did the background of the giraffe chair. Lightly sponge gold paint onto the primed surface. Sponge more toward the outside edges of the table top than in the center to create more visual interest. After sponging the legs, add spots and markings that look like animal skin, again decreasing the size of the marks as they approach the base of the leg. On this table, each leg pattern has a different design and color. You can make up your own fantasy spots or duplicate the ones you see here. Last, paint teddy bear paw prints in different sizes and at random locations on the table top.

17. Allow a week for the paint to dry thoroughly. Then apply three or more coats of polyurethane to the table and chairs, following the manufacturer's directions.

Lace Masking On A Mirror Frame

Any mirror should complement its surroundings, but a free-standing mirror this large establishes its own character and becomes an obvious part of a room's decor. When it's framed in a dark wood, as this one was originally, it looks solemn and heavy. To fit into a room filled with light and antique lace, it had to be changed. The remedy I chose is as quick and easy as it is attractive.

The process is begun by painting your piece of furniture or other object with a base coat. For this softly feminine piece, I chose a creamy off-white. The piece is then covered with lace that has been tacked on with the aid of spray mount. Then it's spray painted with a contrasting color. After the spray paint is dry, the lace is removed to reveal a beautiful result. Add a coat of matte polyurethane to protect the delicate lace pattern, and you're finished. You can easily apply this technique to a masculine chest, doing it all in dark brown and metallic gold, or to a floor cloth for Christmas, using rich burgundy and teal. There's much fun to be had with this trick, and it's so easy to do that you'll want to use it again and again.

Lace can be purchased as a quality second or even by the pound. There were serious flaws in the lace I used, but nothing that would prevent it from working well for this project. Don't use a piece of lace that has value or any that you aren't planning on throwing out after you spray paint it. It's irretrievable.

Lace with a small pattern works best for small projects or projects such as frames, which have small spaces. Lace with larger patterns can be used on big pieces, but you must plan how the lace will look at corners or where drawers meet molding. Of course, the easiest way is to have one solid piece of lace that covers everything. This would be quite feasible on a table top or dresser front.

Once the lace has been sprayed with paint, it can't be reused on another part of the project with good results. The fine mesh clogs with the paint or the spray mount, and the lace becomes difficult to work with once it's stiffened with paint. Make sure that you have enough lace to cover all of the surfaces you want to paint.

The tassel at the top of each side support of the mirror frame is also easy to accomplish. This accent breaks up the lace theme with a little contrast that's not too jarring.

Materials

- Mirror frame or other project
- Masking tape
- Newspaper
- Primer of your choice (see page 10)
- Cream-colored flat oil-based paint
- Acrylic craft paints in small amounts: midnight blue, yellow, pink, blue, light turquoise, opalescent pearl
- White paint pen with medium point
- Lace to cover project
- Spray mount (*not* spray adhesive)
- Light pink spray paint (this mirror took almost three 6 oz/177 ml cans)
- Satin polyurethane

Tools

- #400 wet/dry sandpaper
- 2" (5.1 cm) flat brush
- 1/2" (1.3 cm) flat brush
- #4 round artist's brush

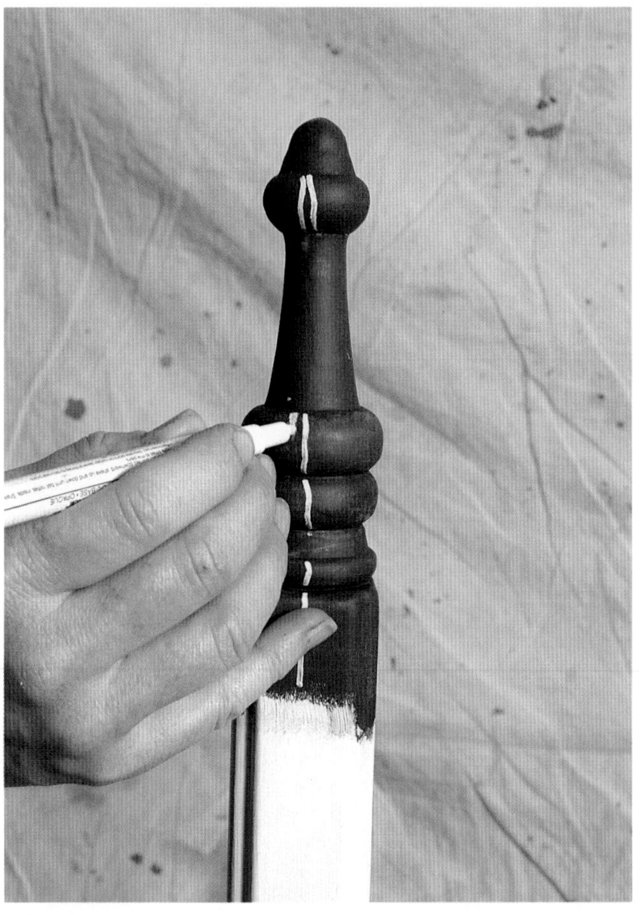

Instructions

1. Dissemble the mirror parts if possible, making sure to note how they go together and putting the nuts and bolts where you can find them later. Cover the glass carefully with paper and masking tape, fitting the tape against the edge of the frame or under it if possible. Alternatively, you can remove the mirror. (This one was cemented in place.)

2. Lightly sand all of the wood that is to be painted. Then use the 2-inch (5.1 cm) brush to prime all of the surfaces of your project. When it's dry, lightly sand the primer coat with the #400 paper and a little soapy water, keeping any drips of water away from the masking tape.

3. When the surface is dry, apply two coats of the base color with the same brush. Allow the paint to dry thoroughly; then sand between coats.

4. After the base color has thoroughly dried and you've lightly sanded it with soapy water and #400 paper, paint on the tassel with the midnight-blue paint and the 1/2-inch (1.3 cm) flat brush. Allow the blue to dry; then use the white paint pen to add the tassel yarns.

5. Tint the white yarns with the #4 brush and acrylic paint washes of different colors. Blend the paint with enough water to obtain a mixture that has the consistency of water. When the washes have dried, apply another coat of wash in yellow to the top areas of the tassel. Finally, paint a light coat of opalescent pearl over the entire tassel to soften its appearance. The colors will still show through the opalescence, but they will be more muted and delicate.

6. Now lay out the lace, and plan where each piece will go. Cut the lace carefully, always considering how portions of the lace pattern will meet one another.

7. Turn the lace over onto newspaper so that the reverse side of the lace faces up, and apply the spray mount. Be careful not use too much spray mount, or you will clog up the lace and the paint won't get through. When the glue has dried, you can test the adhesion of a small section of the sprayed lace by applying it to the mirror frame and smoothing it down. Make sure the edges stay down. If they don't, remove the lace, and spray it again along the edge. Don't apply the lace to the mirror frame until the glue is totally dry, or the glue will come off onto the frame. If this does happen, don't try to remove the glue; just keep dirt away from it. You will be covering it with polyurethane later.

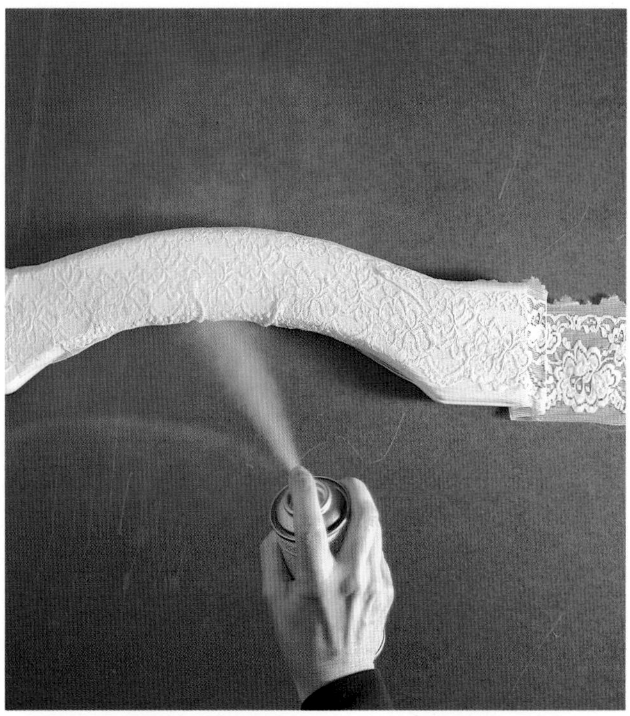

8. When you've positioned all of the lace on one section, you're ready to spray paint. Be sure to apply the lace over the entire section of the project that you plan to paint. Unless you mask it well, you won't be able to keep the paint from going onto the whole area. You should also take pains to protect your work area because the spray will spread throughout your home. It's best to spray paint outdoors when weather permits. Spray the entire piece, making sure all spots are well covered with paint. Be sure to follow all of the manufacturer's directions for using the paint, and shake the can well and often.

9. When the spray paint has dried and you can't see any more bare spots, remove the lace. If there is a glue residue, leave it alone. Any attempts to remove it will more than likely ruin your work.

10. Continue with the rest of your project, following and repeating the steps as necessary. When you've painted the entire project, reassemble it. Now where did you put those nuts and bolts? Lastly, brush on two thin coats of polyurethane.

Rubber-Stamped Insects Decorate an Artist's Box

It's strange how things end up. While our boat was at anchor in the beguiling port of Annapolis, Maryland, I was pleased to discover a gallery filled with marvelous and magical works of art. This visual feast tantalized my already strong need to create, and I rushed off in a fervor to the nearest art supply store to purchase new supplies. There I selected a tempting assortment of tools, materials, and this superb little artist's box. I acquired the box for the express purpose of painting something delightfully magical on it the very next day, or the day after that at the latest.

Time passed, and we sailed away. The box traveled aboard with my husband and me as we drifted, motored, bounced, rolled, and sometimes prayed our way down the intercostal waterway, then made our way back and forth between Florida and the Bahamas. Finally the box arrived here in the mountains of North Carolina, still as naked as it was the day it was purchased.

Now, four years later, the spell of the gallery is broken. The box is painted not with the magic and mystery of the dragon that I'd originally intended, but with a new magic inspired by our glorious herb garden. There, dragonflies, ladybugs, beetles, and butterflies create a bug-filled dreamscape of buzzing, flying, crawling, chirping, and chewing. These creatures maneuvered their way into the garden and onto this box.

The surface design on this bug box is an easy project with a trompe l'oeil flair. The insects are created with rubber stamps; therefore, very little technical or mechanical skill is involved. Rubber stamps are widely available and come in a tremendous variety of sizes and subjects. Choose those that appeal to you, and assemble your own design. To create good trompe l'oeil, use a stamp with a realistic, life-sized image.

The box surface has been dressed up with the texture of an insect net that is easily created with a recycled plastic mesh fruit bag and spray paint. The net has a few recently caught bugs in it to further enhance the realism. When hung on the wall, the finished piece is an interesting shelf on which to display your small objects, and it's sure to draw attention.

The painting of the bugs may be a bit time consuming, so collect the stamps, and add the bugs, just as you would real insects, over a period of time. You can hurry the painting process by coloring the bugs with watercolor pencils and then blending the pencil with the damp point of a brush. You should spray the blended watercolor bugs with matte fixative or coat them individually with polyurethane that isn't water based before continuing.

Materials

- Wooden artist's box
- Primer of your choice (see page 10)
- Cream-colored latex satin enamel
- Small tube of artist's black oil paint
- Mineral spirits
- Cobalt dryer
- Acrylic paints: white, black, several misc. colors and/or watercolor pencils of your choice
- Spray matte fixative or polyurethane*
- Black fine-point paint pen
- Plastic net fruit bag
- 18" x 1/2" (45.7 x 1.3 cm) rope or cord
- Spray mount
- Willow (color) spray paint
- Semigloss polyurethane*

*If you're using both watercolor pencils and paint pens, spray a few light coats of matte fixative over your work to seal it completely before applying any polyurethane. If you're using only paint pens, omit the fixative, and use water-based polyurethane. With watercolor pencils only, use fixative or polyurethane that isn't water based.

Tools

- 1" (2.5 cm) and 2" (5.1 cm) foam applicators
- #400 wet/dry sandpaper
- 6" x 6" (15.2 cm sq.) or larger piece of glass
- Pallet knife
- Ink brayer
- Several rubber stamps of different insects
- #1, #2, and #3 round brushes
- Magnifying glass
- Pencil with sharp point
- Scissors
- Newspapers

Instructions

1. Sand and prepare all surfaces of your box according to the directions on pages 8–10. Then apply two coats of cream latex to all surfaces, inside and out, with the foam applicators. After each coat, sand lightly with #400 paper and a little soapy water. Allow the paint to dry thoroughly.

2. The first of your insects can be stamped on the inside of the box now. Start with a stamp that has the least amount of detail. Using the pallet knife, mix a very small amount of black oil-based paint with a few drops of mineral spirits and a few drops of cobalt drier on the glass square. Continue mixing until you have a consistency similar to India ink (slightly thicker than water).

3. Use the brayer to roll the paint onto the glass in an even, thin coat. Press the stamp firmly into the "ink," then onto a piece of scrap paper. Practice this until you have the technique of even application well in hand. Once you've mastered stamping on scrap paper, "ink" the stamp, and press it firmly and evenly onto the painted surface, being careful not to move it. Place the bug where you won't have any difficulty reaching it later to paint in the details. You can stamp the same image several times in different locations and paint them various colors, or you can create a grouping of the same bug like this collection of ladybugs in the photograph at left below.

4. Remove the paint from the rubber stamp using mineral spirits. Wait until the stamped image has dried thoroughly before painting in the details or stamping another bug close to it. Remember, you don't have to fill the box now; you can add more bugs later, but when you do, be sure to protect the areas that you've already painted.

5. Now comes the fun part. Select a color for your bug that is somewhat translucent so that your black lines will show right through if you misplace a dab of paint. Thin the paint with a little water first. Then, using the appropriately sized brush, dip just the tip of your brush into the paint, and dab it on an area of the insect. Add other colors of similar value, and let them blend for an iridescent look on the wings. You may need to use the magnifying glass for this process. Paint all the like-colored areas before cleaning your brush and moving on to the next color. Should you goof and get the paint where you don't want it, wipe it off with a clean, damp brush tip. If you're using watercolor pencils, shade an area with the pencils, and blend the colors with the dampened tip of a pointed brush. Don't forget to spray fixative on all areas colored by the pencils.

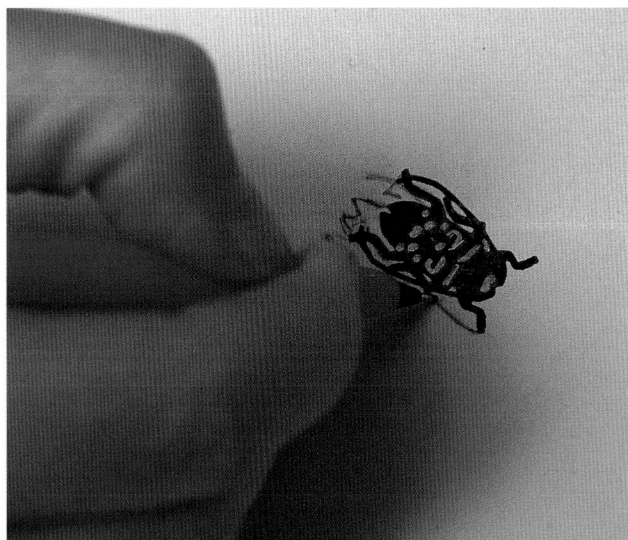

6. When you've painted the entire stamped image to your satisfaction, allow the paint to dry. Then add the shadow. The shadow is very significant, as it imparts a touch of realism that is so important to successful tromp l'oeil. Start by drawing a 1/4-inch (6 mm) border very lightly in pencil along one side and below the lower edge of the insect. See the photograph above. This is your shadow guideline. Then use a #2 brush and a little black water-based paint mixed with water to fill in the penciled border. To look realistic, the shadow should connect to the foot of the bug. Study the example photograph to see how this is done. Do all of the bugs on the inside of the box, following the same procedure.

7. Use the scissors to cut the binding edge off the net bag and to round off the end. Place the net on a large piece of newspaper, and heavily coat one side of the net with spray mount. When the adhesive has dried, position the net, tacky side down, on the top and front of the box, pressing it smooth and secure, and creating a few natural wrinkles as you go. If you're going to hang the box on the wall, as I did, the net pattern shows best if placed on the back and top. (See the photograph on page 54.) Once you have the net positioned, place the rope or cording around the curved edge of the net to form a rim.

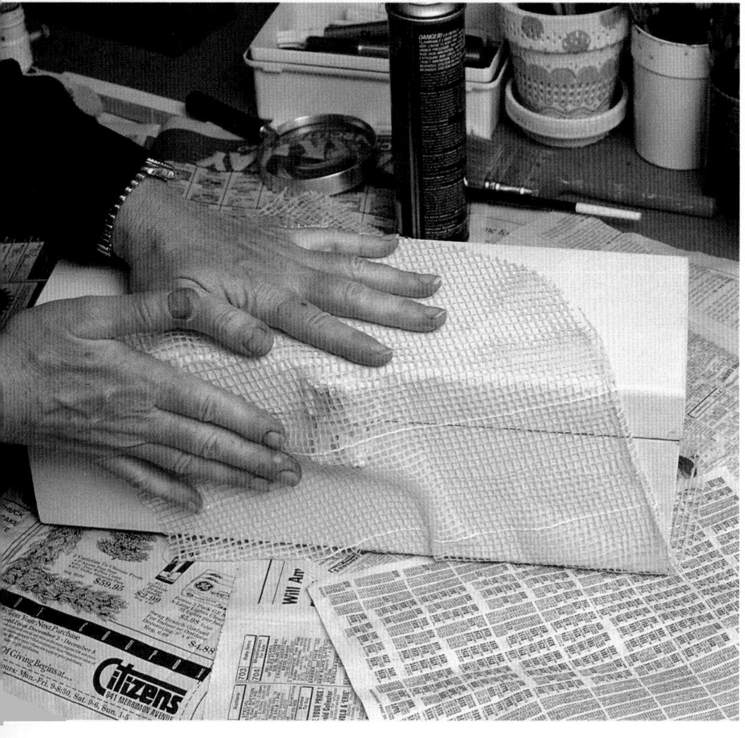

8. Shake the spray paint well, and coat the top and front surfaces of the box with a light application of paint. Wait a few minutes, and repeat the process, making sure that you have total coverage.

9. After allowing the paint to dry, remove the rope. Then turn the box, being careful not to disturb the net, and spray the other side with two coats of paint. When the top has dried, turn over the box, and spray the bottom and ends. After the entire box exterior has dried, remove the net.

10. Use the paint pen to draw the detail on the net rim. (See the photograph on page 54.) You can also add a little shadow to the net rim with a very thin wash of black water-based paint.

11. Plan, position, and paint the insect stamps on the exterior of the box following the procedures above.

12. When you are completely satisfied with your bug collection, finish the box, inside and out, with two coats of the appropriate polyurethane.

Sand Masking, Bird's-Eye Maple, and Punched Tins on an Entertainment Center

The comic puppets Punch and Judy performed long before the notion of television was conceived. However, the old decorative stages where their antics took place so resemble modern TV cabinets that it seemed appropriate for the quarrelsome pair to get top billing on a brand new entertainment center. This project is a hodgepodge of styles, old and new. Punch and Judy duke it out on a pair of punched tins, and the cabinet is painted with bird's-eye maple and other, more abstract patterns.

The tins themselves are actually aluminum flashing available at a hardware or builders' supply store. I used the flashing instead of traditional, authentic tin because the aluminum is readily accessible and much easier to handle. It can be cut with a pair of old scissors, and the holes can be punched with an awl and a little pressure. Punching holes in tin requires heavy exertion with a hammer and nail.

The "aging" of the aluminum tins to give them a rusty looking surface is as easy to accomplish as playing in the sand. The sand is used to mask the tins, and the "rust" is applied from a can of spray paint. This quick process is best done outdoors when the climatic conditions are right.

This project demonstrates a number of techniques that can be used individually on other projects or combined with other techniques. The top of the cabinet has a starry, almost cosmic appearance that looks deep and mysterious. (See the close-up photograph at the end of this chapter. As with many painted finishes, however, this surface can be fully appreciated only by direct viewing; its depth isn't readily visible on the printed page.) The body of the cabinet has a subtle, leatherlike pattern that results from applying a glaze ragged with newspaper. The fanciful bird's-eye maple doors start with the same technique used on the leathery surface and finish with the same methods used for the cosmos top. Even though the techniques are almost identical, the results are very different. The procedure for the tins doesn't involve any of the above techniques, and its use is limited, although I've used the sand masking trick to make lamp shades, window shutters, and fireplace screens.

Materials

- Cabinet with door panels removed
- Shellac for sealer, if necessary
- Primer of your choice (see page 10)
- Acrylic craft paints: fire red, mustard, bright blue, ultra blue, white, brown, peachy beige, red iron oxide, yellow, tangerine, black
- Acrylic medium
- Windsor red and iridescent green artist's oil paints
- Cobalt drier
- Mineral spirits
- Ultramarine blue latex semigloss enamel
- Aluminum flashing at least 1-1/4" (3.2 cm) wider and taller than the panel openings
- Patterns enlarged to size
- Masking tape, 1" (2.5 cm) or wider
- Scrap piece of wood
- Flat black spray paint
- Scrap cardboard
- A bucketful of sand
- Flat red spray paint
- Water-based matte polyurethane
- Newspapers
- Semigloss polyurethane
- A few wood shims
- Tacks

Tools

- #320 and #400 sandpaper
- Clean containers with tight-fitting lids
- Measuring spoons
- 3" (7.6 cm) blunt-end brush for latex paint
- Scissors
- Awl
- Artist's brushes: #4 tapered point, 1/2" (1.3 cm) blunt end, 2" (5.1 cm) blunt end
- Old toothbrush
- Sturdy stick about 12" (30.5 cm) long
- Adjustable fine mist spray bottle
- Tack hammer

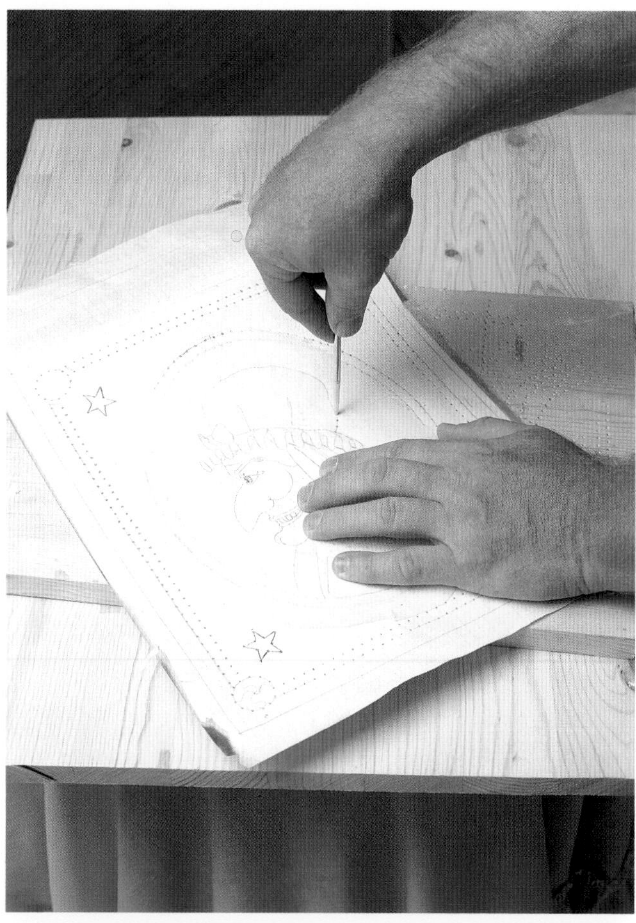

Instructions

1. Start by removing all of the hardware from the cabinet. Then seal all of the knots, and prime the wood surfaces. Sand the primed surface to eliminate any flaws.

2. Before the actual painting of this project begins, mix the glazes and the matte colors that aren't available premixed. For the coral door frames, mix three parts fire red, one part red iron oxide, and ten parts yellow paint. Mix enough paint to cover the door frames inside and out, a small portion of the tins, and some of the trim, and to have enough remaining to make a glaze. The total quantity of coral mixed for this project was 8 ounces (237 ml). Store the paint tightly capped until you're ready to use it.

3. Mix about 10 ounces (296 ml) of the glaze for the faux bird's-eye maple by adding one part of the coral paint mixture to two parts yellow paint and four parts acrylic painting medium. This will produce a pumpkin color. Thin the mixture with a little water, and cap it tightly until ready to use.

4. Mix together one part black paint, two parts acrylic medium, and three parts water. You will need about 4 ounces (118 ml) for a project this size.

5. To prepare the red paint for the cosmos finish, mix six parts oil-based red paint with one part drier, stirring in the drier one drop at a time. Then add enough mineral spirits to make a syrupy mixture. I used a plastic teaspoon (5 ml) as my unit of measure to make enough paint for the top of this cabinet. You may want to wait to mix this paint until you're ready for it, since the oil paint will form a skin. Mix this paint in a small container, and cap it tightly.

6. The iridescent green oil-based paint is mixed the same way as the red, but I used a half-teaspoon (2.5 ml) as the unit of measure.

7. Paint the body of the cabinet with the latex blue paint and the 3-inch (7.6 cm) brush. It will take at least two coats to cover the white primer. The first coat of paint should be thinned slightly with water. When each coat of the latex is dry, lightly wet-sand it with the #320 paper.

8. While the paint on the body of the cabinet is drying, you can start the tins. Cut the aluminum flashing with scissors (not your good ones) to fit the openings in the door frames. Be sure to allow a border of at least 3/4 inch (1.9 cm) to enable you to tack the tins into position on the inside of the doors.

9. Now tape one pattern into position on each piece of aluminum. Working on your scrap piece of lumber, use the awl to press holes through the flashing along the pattern lines about every 1/4 inch (6 mm). This job is easier if you stand over your work.

10. When you've completed the entire pattern on all of the tins, spray them with black paint, following the manufacturer's directions.

11. Allow the spray paint to cure overnight. Then paint the figures with the acrylic paints and the #4 and 1/2-inch (1.3 cm) brushes. You can choose your own colors, or use the ones shown here. You should know before choosing a color, however, that it will be subdued substantially by black spray paint that will be applied over it to antique the surface. The colors you choose should be much brighter than the ones you desire for the final finish.

12. After allowing the painted tins to dry for a day, spread cardboard on the ground outdoors, and place the tins with the image side facing up on the cardboard. Sprinkle sand over the paint, leaving a few small gaps that will appear later as rust spots.

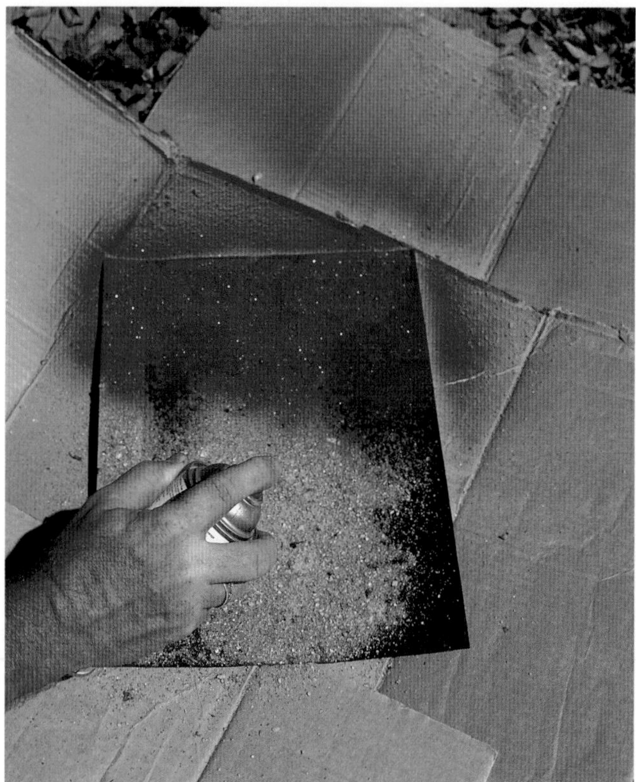

13. Following the manufacturer's instructions, shake the red paint very well, and spray the sand-covered tins. Hold the can away from the surface far enough not to disturb the sand as you're spraying.

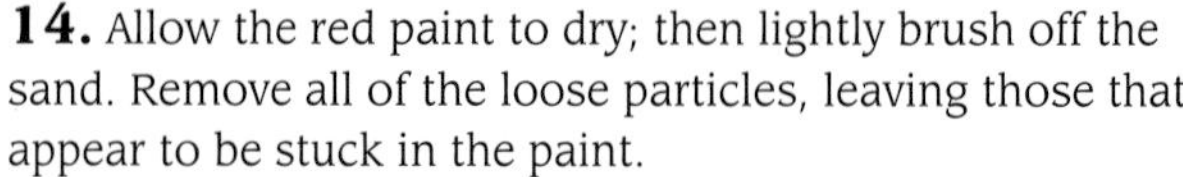

14. Allow the red paint to dry; then lightly brush off the sand. Remove all of the loose particles, leaving those that appear to be stuck in the paint.

15. Now shake the black paint very well, and spray a *light* dusting of paint over the tins. Before the spray comes in contact with the tins, test it on the cardboard to make sure that it's not spitting. Sunlight will make the application of the black paint appear lighter than it is, so take the tins indoors after a very light dusting of paint to make sure that you're not getting them too dark. Set the tins aside to dry thoroughly.

16. To start the faux bird's-eye maple finish, paint both sides of the door frames of the cabinet with the coral paint. Allow the paint to dry 24 hours; then apply a coat of the matte polyurethane.

17. Apply a coat of matte polyurethane to the tins.

18. At least 24 hours after the polyurethane has been applied to the door frames, sand them lightly with the #400 paper. Bunch up eight or more wads of newspaper, using a quarter-sheet for each wad. Place your water-filled spray bottle where it will be handy. Apply a coat of the pumpkin-colored glaze to one section of the door frame, and press the wadded paper into the glaze, removing some of the glaze and creating a pattern. When you've finished one area, glaze another, pat it with paper, and continue until the entire frame is complete. Don't forget the edges. If the glaze starts to dry a little before you've patted it with the newspaper, spray a light mist of water on it. Continue until you've completed both frames.

19. After allowing the glaze to dry, set one frame on a protected work surface so that the front of the frame faces up. Assemble the spray bottle, black glaze, and toothbrush. Now spritz the frame with a light mist of water. Put a small amount of paint into the cap of the glaze container, dip the toothbrush bristles into the glaze, and push them against the edge of the cap toward the wet frame, creating a mist of

dots. The moisture on the frame will cause the specks to diffuse slightly, softening them to look more natural. Continue this way until both doors are rather heavily spotted, allowing some big dots to occur randomly.

20. Allow the spots to dry; then apply one more coat of matte polyurethane. After letting the polyurethane dry overnight, apply a black glaze to the molding detail on the door frames. Wipe off most of the black, leaving a slight residue in the recessed areas to make it look more antique.

21. When this glaze has dried for five days or more, apply two coats of semigloss polyurethane. Let the polyurethane have five additional days to dry and cure. Now turn the frames face down, and tack the tins in place, making sure the tins are square before going beyond the third tack.

22. For the body of the cabinet, wad up enough newspaper to fill a grocery bag. Apply the black glaze to one area at a time, and use the newspaper wads to add texture to it the same way you did the pumpkin color on the door frames. Remove quite a bit of the glaze if you want the blue color to show through strongly.

23. Paint a band of molding at the top and bottom of the cabinet with the coral paint. Repeat the fantasy maple procedure used on the door frames to complete this trim.

24. To create the cosmos top, stand the cabinet on a protected work surface, using wood shims under the feet until the surface is level. Apply masking tape around the outside edge of the top, allowing it to overextend upward by about 3/8 inch (1 cm) to form a barrier to contain a layer of water. Burnish the lower edge of the tape to the cabinet.

25. Assemble the full spray bottle, red oil paint, toothbrush, and stick. Spray the top of the leveled cabinet until it has a layer of water over the entire surface. If the cabinet isn't level, the flow of the water will tell you. Add more shims to correct the problem. Use the toothbrush dipped in

red paint to spray spots of paint onto the wet surface the same way you used the black glaze on the door frames. The red paint won't diffuse, as the black did, as it reacts with the water. Create some large blobs with the red paint by tapping the paint-filled toothbrush against the stick. Add light sprays of water now and then to make the oil paint move around. Using this process, cover the entire top with a red pattern. If the surface starts to dry in any area, spray it with more water.

26. Allow the water to evaporate from the top and the residue of red paint to dry; then repeat the process with the iridescent green paint, applying less of the green than you did the red.

27. Once the cabinet has dried and cured, apply two coats of semigloss polyurethane to the entire box. Between coats, wet-sand the cabinet with #400 paper. Apply two additional coats to the top to increase the illusion of depth in the finish.

Vinegar Painting and Faux Satinwood Revive a Metal File Cabinet

Vinegar painting has been around since the 19th century. It was created by country artisans to emulate the look of fancy graining on furniture and woodwork, but the style quickly shifted from subtlety to boldness. A vigorous application of pattern resulted in pieces that are far more endearing to us now than the wood graining they set out to imitate. The charming effects were added to furniture and woodwork alike and were created with readily available materials: sugar, water, and dry pigment mixed with ale or vinegar. The pigment was optional. A coat of varnish made their work permanent.

The homely, standard-issue file cabinet shown in the photograph on page 66 doesn't lend a bit of charm to any room. It doesn't have much character, and its finish can only be called utilitarian. But look at it now (see the photograph opposite). Personality, color, and visual appeal make this a file cabinet with a story to tell. It's all done with vinegar painting and a simple, new top. The top isn't essential, but it helps break up the sharp corners. The vinegar paint is the secret to the reincarnation of this clunker.

The other great part of the story is the amount of time involved to give this cabinet new life. Not counting drying time, the vinegar painting took one hour for the red and two hours for the yellow (where there is more detail in the graining). If the whole cabinet had been done in vinegar graining, it could have been completed in three days, including applying a base color and a coat of polyurethane. Actual working time would have been less than six hours!

If desired, vinegar paint can be washed away with water after it has dried. This allows you to experiment and make as many changes as your materials and time constraints allow. Once you're happy with the results, a coat of varnish protects the work and makes it permanent.

Satinwood has a beautiful, smooth look to the grain. To imitate it most effectively, oil-based paint is used, which increases the amount of drying time before it can be varnished. The application of the faux satinwood finish on this wooden top takes only a couple of hours. The steps involved are all completed without having to wait for multiple layers to dry.

Materials

- File cabinet or other project
- Metal primer spray paint
- Matte spray paint: 2 large cans peach, 1 can yellow
- Dry tempera or poster paints: gold, red, brown
- Dark-colored vinegar
- Water
- Sugar
- Objects for making patterns: dried strawflower, torn and rolled pieces of grocery bag, small piece of modeling clay, kneaded eraser
- Semigloss polyurethane
- Wooden top made to fit your file cabinet, primed with gesso and sanded to a smooth finish
- Artist's oil paints: yellow ocher, burnt sienna, vermillion, raw umber
- Turpentine
- Cobalt dryer

Tools

- Face mask
- Tarpaulin
- #1 steel wool
- Dust rags
- Tack rag
- Measuring cups and spoons
- Clean containers for mixing
- Straightedge
- Sharp #2 pencil
- 1" (2.5 cm) flat brush
- 2" (5.1 cm) flat brush
- Soft artist's brushes: 2" (5.1 cm) flat, 2 or 3 #6 fans, #4 round, #4 badger blender
- Fine-tooth comb

Instructions

1. While wearing a protective breathing apparatus, prepare your file cabinet for painting by giving it a vigorous rubdown using medium steel wool. The entire exterior surface must be roughened if it's to hold paint. That includes the handles and any other metal part attached to the face of the drawers.

2. When the surface has been sufficiently roughened, the cabinet must be dusted inside and out by wiping it thoroughly with a damp rag. Remove the drawers, and use a tack rag to wipe all surfaces to be painted.

3. Spray painting is best done outdoors if you don't have a well ventilated place for this purpose. Pick a windless, dry day when the temperature conforms to the manufacturer's guidelines on the side of the can. Prime the cabinet, allow it to dry, and follow with your base color. The body of this cabinet was sprayed with peach and the drawer fronts with yellow. Both colors took two coats. Shake the can often and well, or your paint will take forever to dry and will never have the right color consistency. Read and follow all of the manufacturer's directions.

4. Allow the spray paint to dry overnight, or longer if the manufacturer's directions so advise, before you begin the vinegar painting.

5. Mix together 1/4 cup (118 ml) of vinegar, 1/2 cup (236 ml) of water, and 1 teaspoon (5 ml) of sugar until the sugar has dissolved. Place 2 tablespoons (30 ml) of gold, 1 teaspoon (5 ml) of brown, and 1/4 teaspoon (1 ml) of red tempera in a separate, clean container. Add just enough of the vinegar mixture to wet the dry pigment and make a paste. Stir until all of the lumps are out and your paste is smooth; then add a little more liquid, and mix well. Continue to add liquid until the paint is a thick syrup. Cap the paint, and set it aside.

6. Draw a pencil line on each of the drawers to mark a border on all four sides about 1-1/2 inches (3.8 cm) from the edges. This pencil line may show through the paint and look like a seam. This isn't objectionable as long as the line is neatly drawn and doesn't overextend at the corners.

7. Working with the drawer front in a horizontal position, use the smaller flat brush to apply a coat of the gold paint mixture inside the pencil border. Then make impressions in the paint with a dried flower or some other small textured object, experimenting until you find a texture that you like. You'll have about 15 minutes before the paint dries. If it dries before you've finished, wipe off the paint with a damp sponge, and apply another coat. Once you have a satisfactory texture, apply a fresh coat of paint, and begin making impressions in earnest. Start at one corner, and work in a straight line to the adjacent corner, forming one row after another until the entire area inside the border is covered with impressions. Clean up any splashes of paint with a damp cotton swab. Set the drawer aside to dry, and go on to the next one until all of the drawers are decorated in this way.

8. To make the pattern for the border section of each drawer, begin by tearing a long strip from the grocery bag, forming a rough triangle about 2 inches (5.1 cm) wide at the base and about 5 inches (12.7 cm) long. Roll the strip into a tube, starting at the base and working toward the point. The tube should be about 1/4 inch (6 mm) in diameter when you're done.

9. Returning to the first drawer, coat the area outside the pencil line with gold paint. Hold the tube horizontally between your index finger and thumb, and tap it in an up-and-down motion to make impressions with the side of the tube in the paint around the outside border.

10. Set the first drawer aside, and repeat the procedure on the rest of the drawers. When the roll of paper gets soggy, replace it with a fresh tube.

11. Mix the berry-red paint in the same manner as you did the gold. Using the same amount of vinegar, water, and sugar, mix these gradually with 4 tablespoons (60 ml) of red, 2 tablespoons (30 ml) of gold, and 2 tablespoons (30 ml) of brown dry tempera.

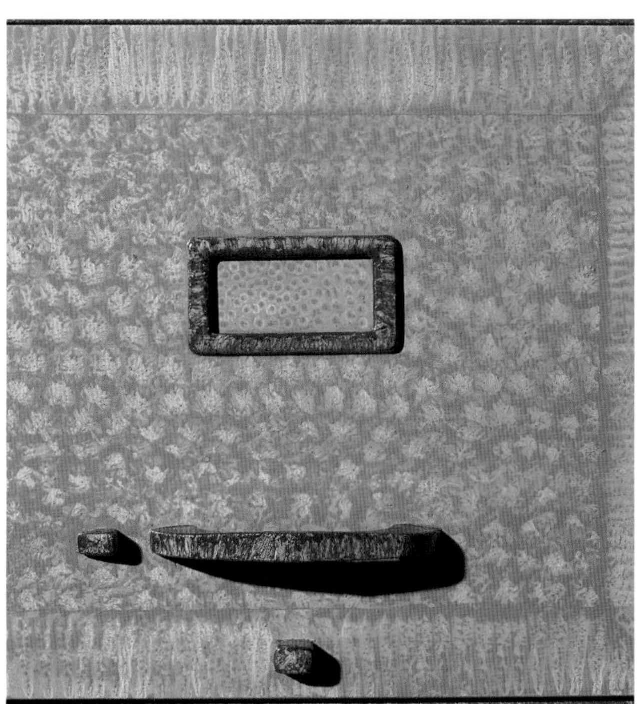

12. With the 1-inch (2.5 cm) brush, carefully apply the red paint to the handles and other attached hardware on the drawer fronts. Then use the paper tube to make impressions in the paint. Try not to get any red paint on the gold areas, or you'll have to touch up the blemishes. Fortunately, the paint is water soluble at this stage. Allow the drawers to dry in a safe place while you apply the red paint to the body of the cabinet.

13. Turn the cabinet on its side, and apply a coat of red paint to the top quarter of the cabinet using the 2-inch (5.1 cm) flat brush. Use a glob of modeling clay or a well softened kneaded eraser formed into an odd shape to make rows of impressions, one next to the other in the red paint. Apply more paint as necessary, and continue with the impressions until the entire side is finished.

14. When the paint dries, turn the cabinet on its back, and apply the red paint to the front edges, being careful not to get any on the freshly painted side. To add texture to the front of the cabinet body, use the 1-inch (2.5 cm) brush. As you're painting, apply a light pressure every 1/4 inch (6 mm) to make an impression. Once the front has dried, protect the finished side with a blanket, and turn the cabinet so that the unpainted side faces up. Complete the painting, and allow the paint to dry overnight. Then apply a coat of polyurethane to all of the painted surfaces.

15. The wooden top for this cabinet, made by a local carpenter, was constructed from 1-inch-thick (2.5 cm) pine that was glued together to make the correct size and trimmed with molding that was tacked and glued to the pine about 1/2 inch (1.3 cm) from the edge. The construction was fairly simple (as you can see in the photograph of the underside), so the cost was minimal.

16. Prime the wooden top with two coats of gesso, sanding after each coat has dried. Then combine four parts yellow ocher, one part cobalt drier, and two parts turpentine to make a glaze. Start by mixing a very small amount of the

turpentine and drier into the oil paint. Do this slowly to smooth out the lumps, and stir in the rest of the turpentine and drier to make a smooth, creamy glaze the consistency of thin latex paint. Apply the paint to the gesso-primed wood with the larger flat brush.

17. While the glaze is wet, create highlights with a dry fan brush, using the tip of the brush to lift a little of the paint in a diagonal pattern on the wood surface. The highlighted areas should be spots about 1 by 4 inches (2.5 by 10.2 cm) in size.

18. Add the wounds in the grain by using the #4 brush and an equal mixture of vermillion, burnt umber, turpentine, and drier. Paint a slightly elongated shape.

19. Next paint the edges of the wound with the point of a good brush moistened with slightly thinned raw umber. Thin the mixture more with turpentine as you get to the elongated tail of the wound.

20. Add a touch of vermillion to the yellow ocher glaze to shift the color subtly. Wet your largest fan brush with water, and dip its tips into the yellow ocher and vermillion glaze. Then comb the brush to separate the hairs into clumps. Lightly drag the brush over the glazed surface, creating grain lines that bump up in an arch over the highlights and wiggle back and forth in tiny jerks in the spaces between.

21. Wait five days or longer after applying the glaze; then finish the satinwood with two coats of polyurethane applied with the 2-inch (5.1 cm) brush. At this time, you may wish to apply another coat of varnish to the entire cabinet.

Painted Marquetry on a Fox Lover's Box

The love of equestrian sports enticed my husband and me to visit some horse owning friends in Ottawa, Canada, where we enjoyed the dazzle and thrill of a traditional fox hunt. In this hunt, they don't actually pursue and kill a fox; instead, the master of the hunt creates a trail of fox scent for the dogs, horses, and riders to follow over hill and dale. It may not be as electrifying as hunting the real thing, but the fox likes it.

We couldn't help but be intrigued, then fall in love with their imaginary quarry, the beautiful fox, whose memorabilia was everywhere in sight. Knowing this, our friend presented us with a fox-head stirrup cup that we treasure. A few other foxy things have also come our way, so I designed this box in homage to the free spirit of the fox and to provide a place in which to display the items.

The border on the lid of the box features a series of abstract fox heads painted to resemble inlaid wood. When crafted in wood, this technique is called marquetry. *It involves piecing together different kinds of wood veneer to create a decorative pattern. The veneers are glued to a soft wood base, and the pieces are held in place under pressure until the glue is dry. The process requires skill and hard work, but the end results are often quite breathtaking.*

Marquetry patterns are frequently very geometric, making the imitation of the real thing a fairly simple project to duplicate in paint. No drawing skill is necessary; you need only a straightedge and a pencil. The pattern, cut to function like a stencil, is attached firmly to the wood. Then various sections of the wood are exposed and stained in turn. The faux inlay pattern shown here could easily be adapted for a picture frame, a table top or edge, a lamp base, or a border for a wood floor.

The three-dimensional fox head was molded from a cast metal doorstop. The mold was made of plastic modeling clay and cast in water putty. After it hardened, the molded piece was trimmed using a craft knife. You may not have a fox head from which to cast, but any other favorite animal such as a horse or dog would work just as well.

This project requires no more technical skill than earlier projects in the book, but it does take more time and patience because of the complexity involved. In addition to the inlay and molding techniques, this project includes faux rosewood and satinwood (described in detail on pages 148–49 and 67–68, respectively).

The materials and tools lists are for the entire project as you see it here. If you intend to do only the inlay or some other portion, be sure to read all of the directions and choose only the supplies that apply.

Materials

- Box or other wooden project
- Clear, self-adhesive plastic
- Several copies of pattern, sized to fit your project
- Spray mount
- Rubbing alcohol
- Acrylic craft paints: candy bar brown, antique gold (not metallic), black
- Black paint pen
- Black fine-line waterproof marker
- Nonhardening plastic modeling clay
- 1/2 lb. (227 g) rock-hard water putty
- Gesso
- Artist's oil paints: white, burnt sienna, vermillion, alizarin crimson, burnt umber, black, permanent green deep, yellow ocher, raw umber
- Turpentine
- Cobalt drier
- Water-based semigloss polyurethane
- Glass eyes for animal head (available at craft stores)
- Wood glue
- Mahogany stain
- Mineral spirits
- Noncuring plastic masking tape (see page 15)
- Orange shellac
- 2" (5.1 cm) wood screw

Tools

- Sandpaper: #240, #320, and #400
- Pencil with eraser
- Craft knife
- Straightedge
- Cotton swabs
- Brushes: 1/4" (6 mm) flat, 1/2" (1.3 cm) flat, 1-1/2" (3.8 cm) flat
- Artist's brushes: #4 pointed, #4 fan
- 3-dimensional object to mold
- Old toothbrush
- Scissors
- Sheet of grid paper
- 2 push pins
- Nonstretching string

Instructions

1. Start your project early on a day that you can devote entirely to it. Once you've sanded your box lid thoroughly, starting with the coarsest and ending with the finest paper, the first step is to cover the lid with the self-adhesive plastic. If the plastic is left on too long, its adhesive will cure, making it difficult to remove. This is less likely to occur if you can remove it the same day that it's applied.

2. After you've covered the lid and smoothed out the plastic, making sure that you have good adhesion throughout, position your pattern on top. Cut the pattern and tape it together as necessary to make it one solid pattern that fits your project. When the pattern is aligned properly, make a few pencil marks to indicate its position on the plastic, and remove the pattern. Apply spray mount to the back of the pattern, and reposition it on the box, matching up the pencil marks.

3. Using the craft knife and straightedge, cut the fox-head inlay pattern on all of the lines. Then remove only the black areas of the pattern and the plastic underneath. Let the

sharp knife blade do the work, not brute strength and pressure, or you will cut too deeply into the box surface. Make sure that you remove all the plastic, as it may be difficult to see. If you find bits of gum still clinging to the wood when you remove the plastic, lift them with a cotton swab moistened with rubbing alcohol.

4. Using the 1/2-inch (1.3 cm) brush lightly dipped into the brown acrylic paint, fill in the areas that you have removed. Use an up-and-down tamping motion with the brush to get the paint well into the corners. The paint should be the consistency of heavy syrup. If it's too thin, it may bleed under the plastic.

5. When the paint is dry, remove the remaining portion of the fox-head pattern and the plastic underneath.

6. Apply the antique gold, slightly thinned with water, over the entire fox pattern, including the brown portions. The gold is translucent and will allow the brown to show through.

7. Using the straightedge and craft knife, cut away the rest of the pattern border and the plastic underneath. Check for any adhesive residue, and remove it with the alcohol and cotton swab. Then outline the fox-head inlay parts using a straightedge and a black fine-line, waterproof marker.

8. Paint in the border with the acrylic black and the #4 pointed brush.

9. Remove all of the self-adhesive plastic from the box lid, and clean up any gooey residue with the rubbing alcohol. Try not to get any alcohol on the areas that you've painted or marked because they may smear or bleed. This step should be completed on the same day that you applied the plastic. If you have a little problem, don't panic; you can always clean it up with turpentine and a cotton swab and, if necessary, a tiny piece of sandpaper.

10. Molding the fox head doesn't relate strictly to painting furniture, but the technique comes in very handy when a piece of decorative molding is missing. Remove a similar piece of molding that you do have, and press it into modeling clay. After carefully removing the molding from the clay, fill the cavity with rock-hard water putty. Allow the putty to dry, remove the clay mold, and your replacement molding can be glued into position and finished.

To mold the fox head, a slightly different procedure is used to compensate for the depth of the figure. The clay is applied to the object (in this case, a doorstop) in small pieces and smoothed on until the mold is built up to cover the entire fox head to a depth of at least 1/2 inch (1.3 cm).

11. After you've finished building up the mold, carefully remove it from the object, taking care not to stretch the clay and distort the mold. Then mix the rock-hard water putty according to the manufacturer's directions, and pour it into the mold.

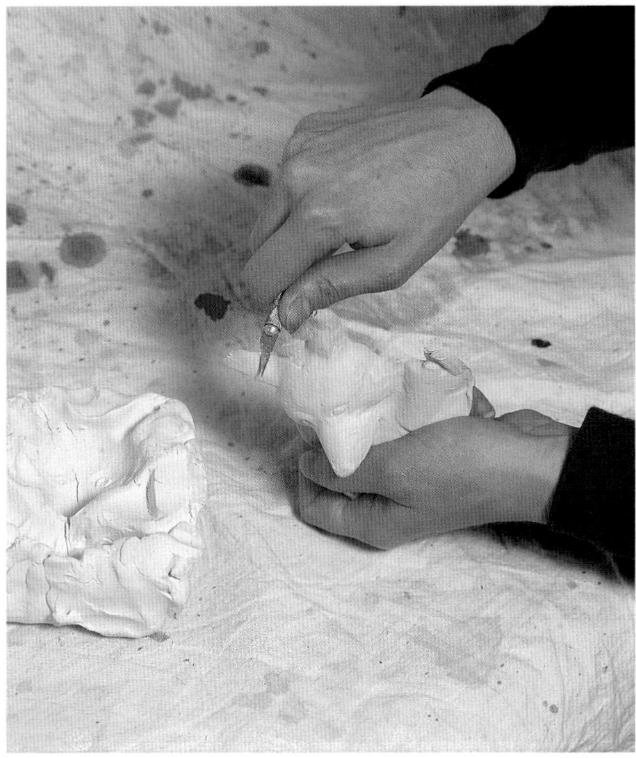

12. Allow adequate time for the putty to dry (two days) before removing your casting from the mold. The excess putty is easily carved away with the craft knife. Use the tip of the craft knife to make small hollows in the eyes to hold the glass inserts. Make sure the glass eyes fit and look natural, but don't glue them in place until the fox head is completely painted and sealed with the polyurethane.

13. Get rid of any rough edges at the base of the casting by sanding it lightly. If you're not happy with your cast, then make another one. It's easy and doesn't take long.

14. Complete instructions for painting faux rosewood are provided on pages 148–49. The same steps are repeated here in miniature on the fox head. To review these steps briefly, the fox is painted first with gesso, then with a mixture of white, alizarin crimson, burnt sienna, vermillion, cobalt drier, and turpentine. When this glaze is dry, add black graining lines, and blend them as necessary according to the directions on page 149, but using smaller brushes.

15. After you've applied two coats of polyurethane to the fox head, use the wood glue to attach the eyes.

16. Allow the inlay border to cure for five days before continuing with the top. To protect it while working on the interior and bottom portion of the box, tape paper over the box lid.

17. The inside of the box is a great place to practice faux rosewood before you do the outside surface. A faster solution for the interior would be to paint or stain it. This box interior has a combination of paint and rosewood graining.

First prime the entire interior with gesso. Then paint it with a mixture of white, alizarin crimson, burnt sienna, vermilion, cobalt drier, and turpentine. Consult page 148 for the proportions. After the base color is dry, apply the graining according to the instructions on page 149. Then add green highlights as accents.

18. The wood grain on the exterior of the box was irregular, unattractive, and definitely in need of some help. The method used for these surfaces is faster and requires fewer materials than rosewood graining, and it's convenient to use on larger projects. However, it's not as elegant as the rosewood.

First wipe the box with the mahogany stain, following the manufacturer's directions for stain application. After the stain has dried, thin a little of the black oil-based paint with mineral spirits. Using a 1/4-inch (6 mm) flat brush, paint a black line that follows the existing grain. Make the line thicker in some places, and press a pencil eraser into the thickest area to form a knotlike shape. Soften the entire length of the black line by pulling a fan brush perpendicularly down through the lower edge of the grain. Repeat this procedure to form more grain lines to cover the entire base of the box. Allow one side to dry before continuing on to the next.

19. Use the thinned black paint to shade the area around the hinges slightly. Then use an old toothbrush to speckle the same black glaze onto the entire surface of the box. To make sure that your spatters are even, practice this step on scrap material first.

20. Let the stained surface dry and cure thoroughly before applying a coat of polyurethane.

21. Once the inlay pattern has had a chance to cure properly, you're ready to finish the box lid. Cover the painted border with the plastic masking tape, cutting the ends of the tape to fit tightly against the unfinished wood. Then burnish the tape against the wood.

22. Apply one coat of shellac over the entire lid, tape included. Then apply two coats of gesso to the rest of the lid, sanding gently between coats.

23. To make the oval in the center of the lid, lay it out first on a sheet of grid paper. Starting with a general idea of the size of oval that you'll need, draw a center line vertically and horizontally on the grid paper. Then mark the width and height of the oval along these axes. Place the two push pins an equal distance from the center point on the horizontal or longest axis. The more oblique the oval, the farther apart the push pins will be located. You'll have to experiment with the distance between the push pins and the length of the string to get it just right. Tie the non-stretch string into a loop just long enough to allow a pencil point to reach the farthest vertical and horizontal ends of the axis at the edge of the oval while the string is taunt around the push pins. Then draw the oval with your pencil, using the string as a guide.

24. Once you've drawn a satisfactory oval on the grid paper, it's time to replicate it on the box lid. Find the center of the box lid and match it up with the center of your oval on the grid paper. Square up the paper, and press the pins through the two holes in the grid and into the box. Remove the pins and grid; then reinsert the pins, with the string in place, in the lid. Finally, draw the oval directly on the lid using the pencil.

25. Following the instructions for satinwood on pages 67–68, paint the inside of the oval. The close-up photograph above shows what the satinwood should look like when it is finished.

26. Paint the area between the oval and the inlay border according to the instructions for rosewood on pages 148–49. Then carefully remove the masking tape from the border.

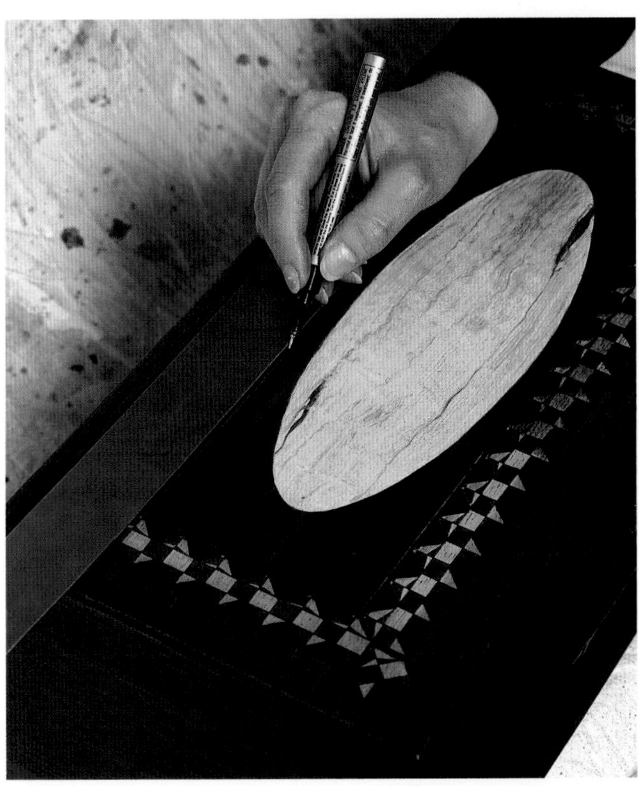

27. Allow several days for the paint to dry and harden. Using a straightedge and paint pen, outline the inlay.

28. Allow a week for the paint to cure. Then apply several coats of protective water-based varnish, letting the varnish dry between coats and sanding it very lightly with #400 paper.

29. To finish the top, position and glue the fox head on the center of the box lid. This head was positioned for hanging the box on the wall. When the glue is dry, drill a tap hole through the lid and into the center of the fox head. Mark the correct depth for this hole first with a piece of tape on your drill bit, since you don't want to drill through the animal's face. Insert the wood screw with a bit of glue, and paint the screw head to camouflage it.

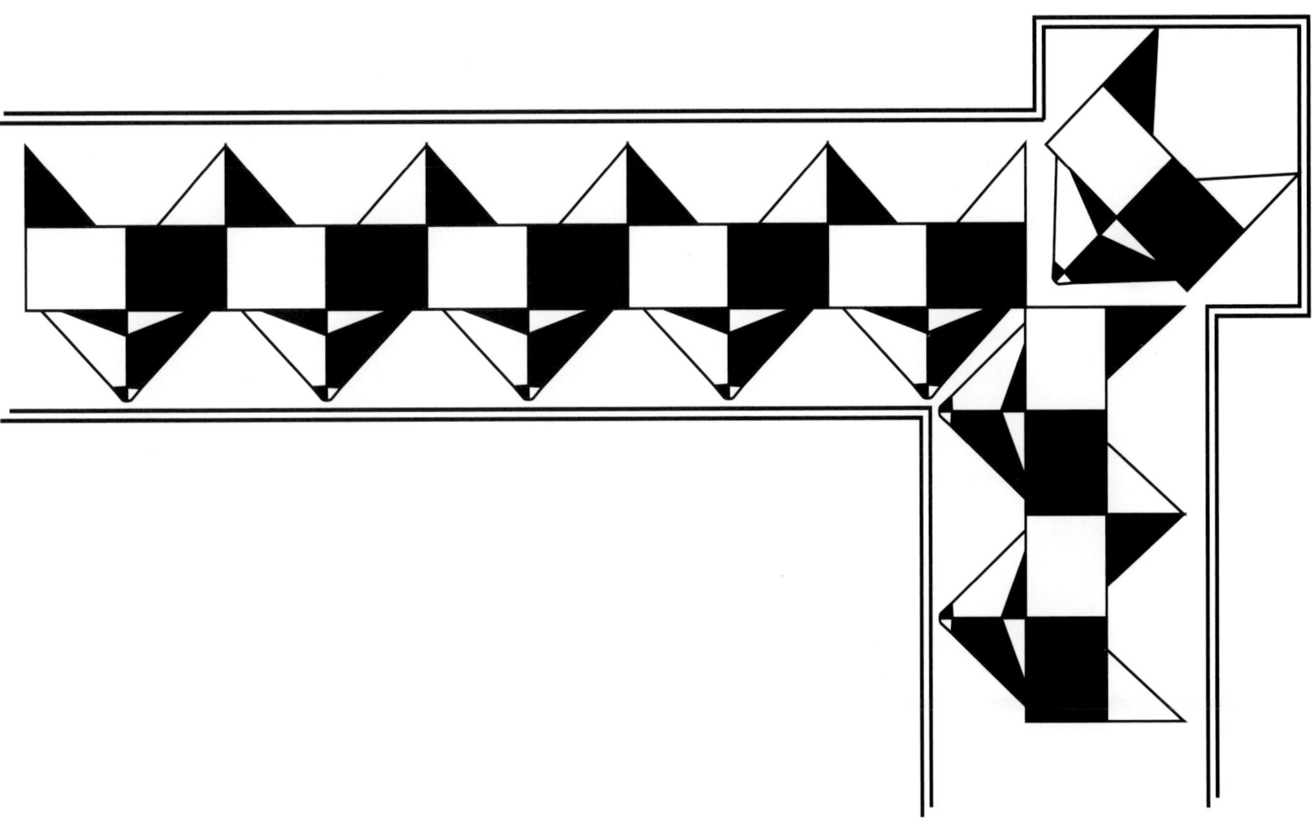

CONTEMPORARY FOLK-ART CHAIRS

These chairs are the perfect project for someone who doesn't like to plan everything ahead. The colors are painted in an impromptu fashion, and the decorations are added spontaneously. The only aim is to balance the color, and the only restriction is not to repeat the same color combinations in the same place. Order is enforced by the limitations of the pallet.

When I started these chairs, the most distressing problem was what to do about the seats. Their tattered condition verged on the hazardous, and they had to be repaired. My husband, Dick, came to the rescue by weaving new rush seats. He found the materials, a sheet of instructions, and a few simple tools at a local craft store. In a matter of a few hours, each seat looked brand new.

Materials

- Chairs
- Primer of your choice (see page 10)
- Acrylic craft paints: dusty mauve, medium ultra blue, old parchment, rain-forest green, palomino
- Paint pens (optional): blue, red, yellow
- Water-based polyurethane

Tools

- Fine sandpaper
- Artist's brushes: 1/4" (6 mm), 1/2" (1.3 cm), 1" (2.5 cm) flat, 2" (5.1 cm) flat, #4 round

Instructions

1. Apply a white primer to the chairs, and lightly sand them before adding the acrylic paint. This step provides a bonding agent between the paint and the chair. The chairs will be bumped around a bit in their new life, and polyurethane alone won't prevent the acrylic from being knocked off wood that isn't primed.

2. Experiment with your pallet before you begin to paint. To achieve the simple harmony of these chairs, choose a group of about five or six colors that are fairly close in value and intensity. Value is the relative lightness or darkness of a color, and intensity is the degree of purity (a color becomes less intense when mixed with another color). In other words, paint pastels with pastels, muted pastels with muted pastels, brights with brights, and so on. These chairs are painted in muted pastels. If they had been painted in dusty mauve and bright orange, with accents of black, grass green, and grey, they would have an entirely different character and not all that much harmony. (Disharmony, though unsettling, is sometimes desirable and exciting. If you want a piece of furniture that will hold the limelight, paint it colors that are jarring when combined.)

An alternative to creating your own pallet is to match the colors from a piece of fabric that will be in the same room as the chairs. Take your fabric swatch to the craft store to select the paint. There are so many colors available in acrylic craft paints that you probably won't have to do any color mixing on your own.

3. Once you've established your pallet, test it on a piece of scrap lumber or cardboard. Paint sections of each of the main colors, placing different combinations next to each other until all of the possible combinations have been tried. Check to make sure that you like all of these combinations. If not, adjust the intensity or value of a color by adding a tiny bit of black or white paint to the offending color until you're pleased with your pallet mixture.

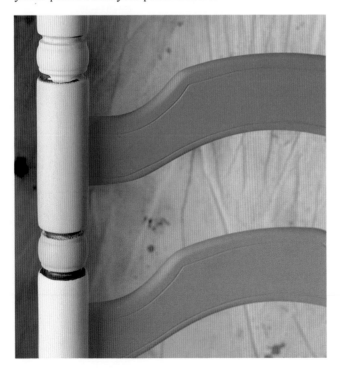

4. Next attack the chairs with the 1-inch (2.5 cm) brush and your favorite color from the pallet. Paint large sections of this color at different locations on the chairs. If your chairs have no breaks from section to section as these chairs do, create your own breaks by joining two main color sections with a decorative line painted in an accent color. (This technique was used on the connecting leg rails of these chairs.) Don't worry too much about neatness; the accent color will cover any imperfections where two colors come together.

5. When you've painted all the solid large blocks of color, apply the accents from an established, predetermined pallet that's designed to be a little bold. These accent colors should express themselves at different and spontaneous locations determined by your whim; their function is to join together two harmonious colors and to add a little zing. If you feel more secure with a pen rather than a brush, you can use the paint pens for the application of accent lines and dots.

6. Once you've finished with the accent colors, it's time to apply your own impetuous, decorative markings. These decorations are designed by your imagination and formed by the different shapes of paint brushes, pencil erasers, and cotton swabs. Try not to plan their placement ahead of time, but do test them on a piece of scrap material before you put them on your chairs. When you apply your brush to the wood, be generous with your markings. The more decorations you add, the more special the chairs will become.

The photos opposite show some simple decorative marks that you can make with a brush and others that you can do with a cotton swab. Experiment with the brushes. Just pressing the side of the #4 round brush flat against the painted surface can give you a leaf shape, a triangle, a dot, or a star burst, depending on the angle and the pressure of the application. A paint-loaded 1-inch (2.5 cm) brush makes an easy wavy line. Don't try to make any perfect lines or marks; keep everything in the casual style intended, and you'll end up with chairs that are uniquely yours.

7. The back of the chairs shouldn't be ignored. Chairs are often pushed under a table, and the back is all that you see. Paint them by drawing on your own inspirations. The series of images on the backs of these chairs was inspired by the earth, sea, and sky.

8. To finish the chairs, use the 2-inch (5.1 cm) brush to paint each of the seats with one of the dominant colors. Alternatively, you may choose to leave the seats natural. After all of the paint has dried, apply two good coats of polyurethane to all surfaces, including the seats.

Stenciled Dining Table with a Whimsical Base

When it was first brought home, this solid maple table looked utterly forlorn and in need of some good cheer (see the photograph below). And what better way is there to get cheered up than to have a new set of clothes and a make-over? The top of the rejuvenated table has been painted with a tablecloth that will always stay in position and can be wiped to a clean glisten with a damp cloth. The pattern is that of an informal, pastel-colored quilt—a totally casual set of new clothes. The quilt pattern suggests a country style, but the more whimsical base makes this a distinctly contemporary folk-art piece.

The quilt pattern is stenciled onto the refinished maple top so that the beauty of the wood can show through, not only as a background, but also as a color in the quilt pattern. Located in the center of the table where the least amount of wear will take place, the relatively small size of the pattern keeps it from being intrusive. The top pattern is kept simple to harmonize with the busy pattern of the base, and the color palette is maintained throughout to unite the two different designs.

This table design is perfect for the lighthearted feel of a vacation home or the living space for the young at heart. Its cheerful colors and playful designs are keyed for someone who doesn't take furnishings all that seriously. This color scheme can be carried throughout your entire home, or you can alter the colors to complement your other furnishings.

Materials

- Wooden table
- Paint and varnish remover
- Artist's oil paints: yellow ocher, vermillion
- Turpentine
- Liquin
- Satin polyurethane
- Pattern enlarged to fit your table
- Waxed stencil paper large enough to cut each pattern to size, allowing a border of at least 1-1/2" (3.8 cm) around each pattern
- Masking tape
- Acrylic craft paints: old parchment, palomino, dusty mauve, medium shade of ultra blue, light shade of rain-forest green, miscellaneous accent colors

Tools

- Plastic gloves
- Rags
- #4/0 steel wool
- #320 and #400 wet/dry sandpaper
- Pallet or piece of glass edged with several layers of masking tape
- Pallet knife
- 2-1/2" (6.4 cm) flat brush
- #2 pencil with eraser
- Long metal straightedge
- Craft knife with new blades
- Grease pencil
- Stencil brushes in several sizes from 1/2" to 1-1/4" (1.3 to 3.2 cm) diameter
- Putty knife
- Cotton swabs
- Artist's brushes: 1/4" (6 mm), 1" (2.5 cm), 2" (5.1 cm) flats; #4, #6 rounds

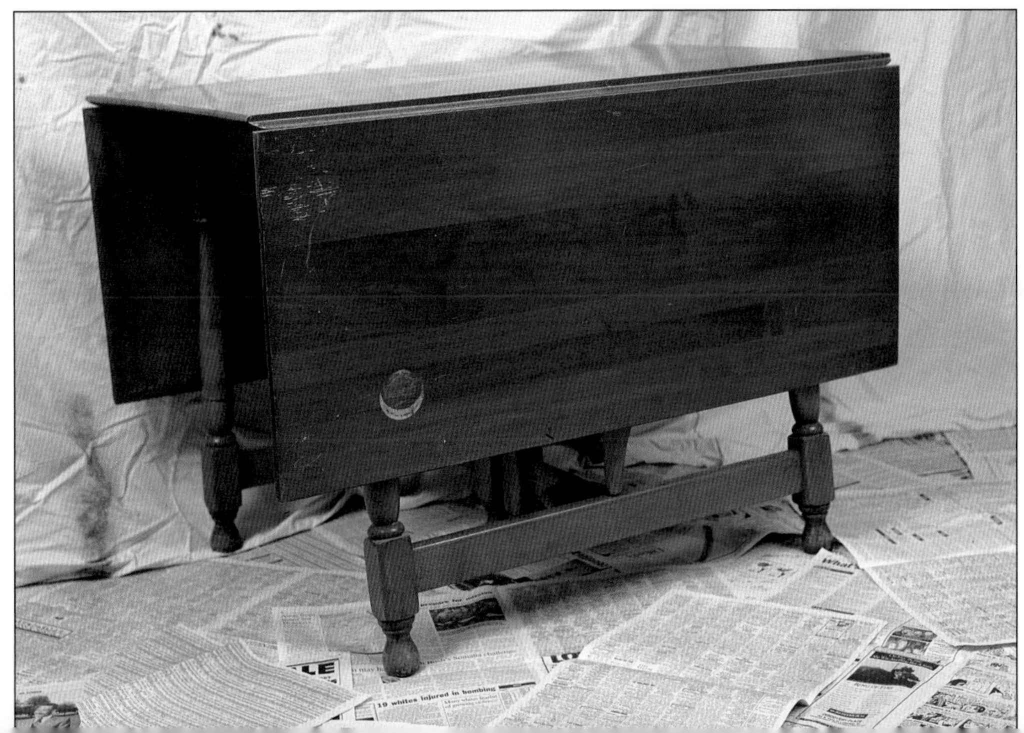

Instructions

1. Begin by stripping all of the old varnish off the table top using a commercial stripper, steel wool, and rags. See page 9 for more information on stripping wood. If the wood is stained from use, brush on a three percent solution of hydrogen peroxide, and allow it to soak out the stains. Then rinse and wipe the surface with a damp sponge. Sand the base of the table with #320 paper and some soapy water to roughen the surface for painting.

2. None of the commercially available stains had quite the color I wanted, so I made a homemade glaze with a little paint right out of the tubes. To duplicate my blend, first rub the top with a mixture of four parts yellow ocher, one part Liquin, and four parts turpentine. On your palette, mix the oil color and the Liquin together with a pallet knife. Then slowly work the turpentine into the mixture, rubbing out any globs of paint with the pallet knife. Apply the ocher glaze to the table top, and wipe away any excess.

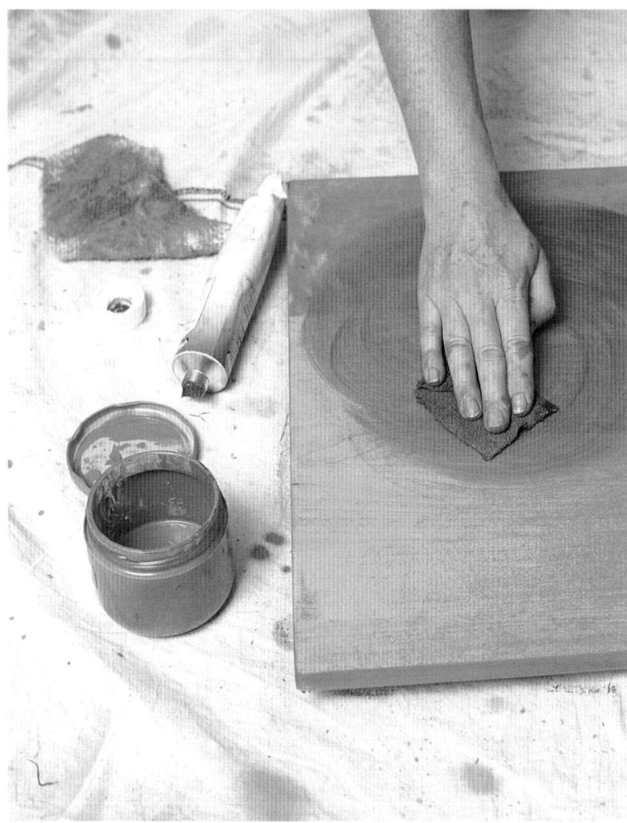

3. Next wipe on a dab of vermillion with a splash of turpentine. Instead of mixing the turpentine and vermillion in a container, mix them right on the wood surface with your rag. It's faster and easier. For a finish that's less red, add more turpentine. Allow this stain to sit for five minutes; then wipe off any excess paint. Check around the edges for any drips or excess color.

4. Following the same procedure, the underside of the table leaves need to be stained and finished as well. (They show when the table is folded.) Allow the stain on the table top to dry thoroughly—about five days—before turning the table leaves face down to work on the backside. Coat the back of the leaves with polyurethane, and when the polyurethane has dried thoroughly, turn the table top over. Now apply a coat of polyurethane to the entire face of the table. After the varnish has dried, rub it down with fine #4/0 steel wool.

5. During the time spent waiting for the varnishes to dry, you can cut the stencil. The pattern shown is a quarter of the total quilt design. Each quarter repeats the same geometric design, but all of the colors from one quarter to the next need not be all the same. To cut the stencil, first place the sized pattern on a drawing surface, taping it down. Tape the waxed stencil paper in position, and trace the pattern using a pencil and straightedge. Make sure to leave a 1-1/2-inch (3.8 cm) border of stencil paper, or the stencil mask will be too floppy when you use it. Trace all the stencil patterns in this way.

6. Cut out the stencil patterns using a metal straightedge and a craft knife with a fresh, sharp blade. Take care not to overcut the corners. As you cut, protect the pattern area that will become part of the stencil by covering it with the straightedge. Watch your finger tips. They can easily be cut with a fresh blade. If you feel any drag in the blade or have difficulty getting a clean cut, replace the blade. After you cut each stencil pattern, label it with its sequence number and correct colors. This will prevent confusion later.

7. Find the center point on your table top, and mark it lightly with the grease pencil. Find the center point (from side to side) on one table leaf, and mark it also. Then draw a line connecting the two points. Position stencil #1 on the table top, putting the center corner of the stencil on the center point of the table top and the diagonal corner of the stencil on the line. Tape the stencil down securely.

8. Stenciling is done with a brush that is almost dry, and the paint is applied with an up-and-down tamping motion. Small specks of paint are released onto the surface, creating a soft matte bloom of paint. The brush is never pushed or pulled across the surface because that would smudge and destroy the look of the pattern and force paint up under the edge of the stencil. Tamping the color is usually started at the center of the cut-out design and worked toward the outer edge, causing the color to be a little darker in the middle. For this quilt pattern, the opposite was done; a darker edge and lighter center gives the geometric shapes the illusion of puffiness.

9. Remove your grease pencil marks with a soft cloth. To start painting with the stencil, place a puddle of blue paint on the pallet, and dip the flat bristle ends of the largest stencil brush into the paint. Tamp the end of the brush onto your pallet until no blobs of paint are released by the brush. Holding down the edge of the stencil with the putty knife, begin tamping the paint onto the table top. When your brush runs out of paint, reload, tamp it first on the pallet, and, when the amount of paint seems right, continue to tamp in the design until the entire cut-out area is covered with paint. This coverage needn't be opaque, but it should be even. Some background tone showing through the paint may be desirable, depending on your preferences.

10. When you've finished all of the blue on this stencil, detach the stencil, and check your work for sharpness and leaks. If there are any leaks, clean them with a water-

dampened cotton swab, using the straightedge to protect the fresh paint. Rub the cotton swab back and forth over the unwanted paint and against the straightedge until the paint lifts. Using the straightedge as a guide for the cotton swab will help you maintain the sharpness of your stenciling.

11. Measure, mark, and draw another center line down the next quarter of the table, and move the stencil to that section, aligning the stencil as you did previously. If necessary, adjust the position of the stencil so that the edges of the large blue squares in the center of the quilt butt up against each other. In the end, the four squares will make one large, solid blue square with a second color laid over the top.

12. Once you've completed all the sections of stencil #1, continue with stencil #2 and the parchment-colored paint. Align the eight-point star in the small blue box, the outside mark with the corner of the small blue box, and the line with the edge of the large blue box.

13. Tamp the parchment paint into the star and diamond areas. Then move the stencil to the next quarter of the design, and repeat the procedure until all four areas are completed.

14. The third stencil has two colors, mauve and green. Position it and tamp in the colors, covering the blue and parchment paint in some cases, until all four sections are complete. Be sure to use the putty knife to hold down the edges of the stencil to ensure a sharp image.

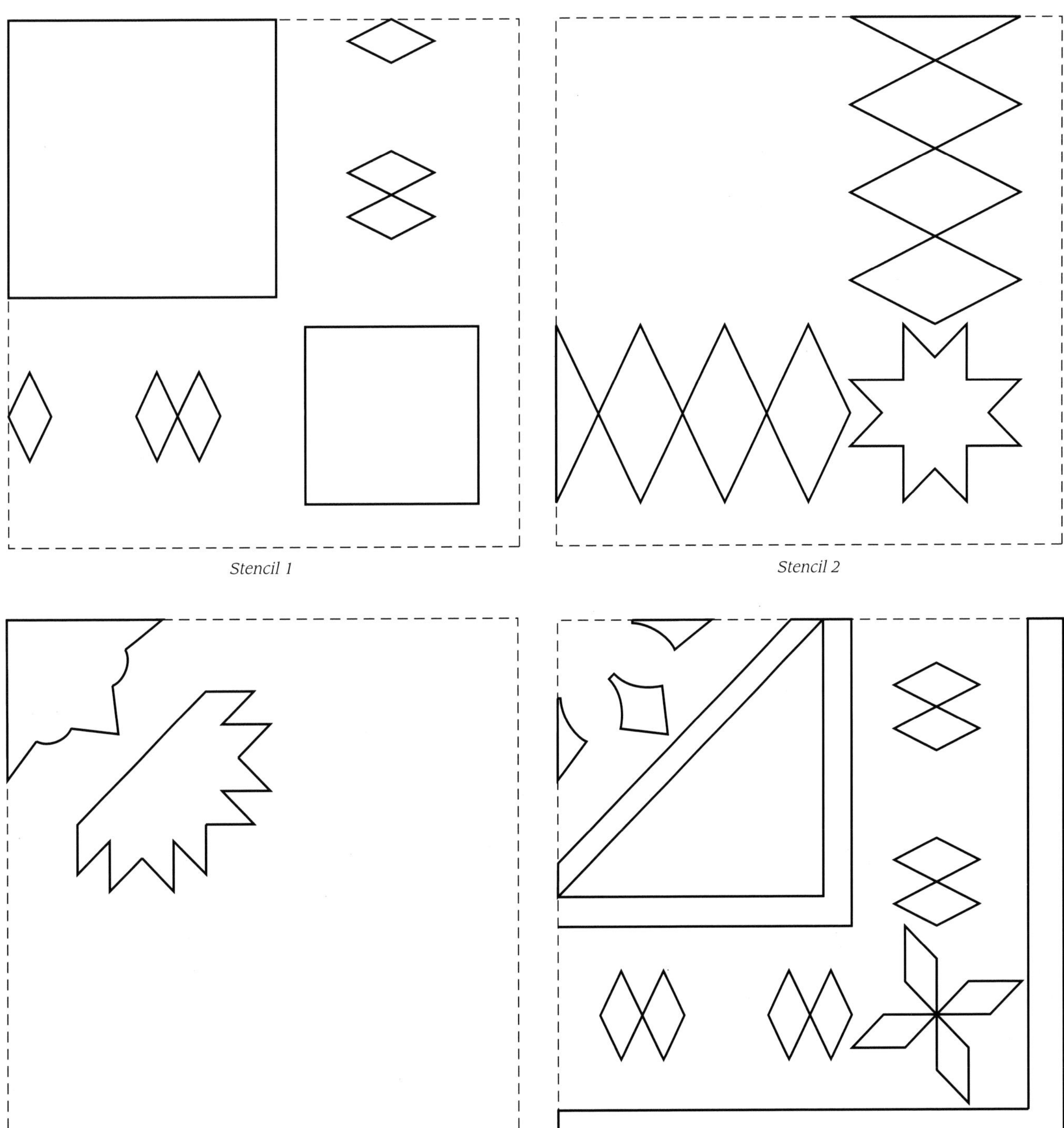

Stencil 1

Stencil 2

Stencil 3

Stencil 4

15. Continue with the rest of the stencils in the same manner until the design is complete. After letting the paint dry for five or more days, apply three coats of polyurethane. Allow the individual coats to dry, and rub them lightly with steel wool. Then wipe the surface thoroughly with a soft, lint-free rag before applying the next coat. Don't use steel wool on the top coat.

16. The base of the table is done following the same procedure used for the chairs in the previous chapter.

First a pallet of major colors is established. In this case, the colors used for the table top are repeated on the base. The placement of each color and the patterns for each section are chosen spontaneously. Select large areas, and paint them with solid colors. Attempt to keep the colors somewhat balanced, but varied on each leg. Next the smaller sections are painted with accent colors, again at random and from a brighter but established pallet. Lastly, add decorations using the #4 artist's brush, 1/4-inch (6 mm) flat brush, pencil eraser, and cotton swabs.

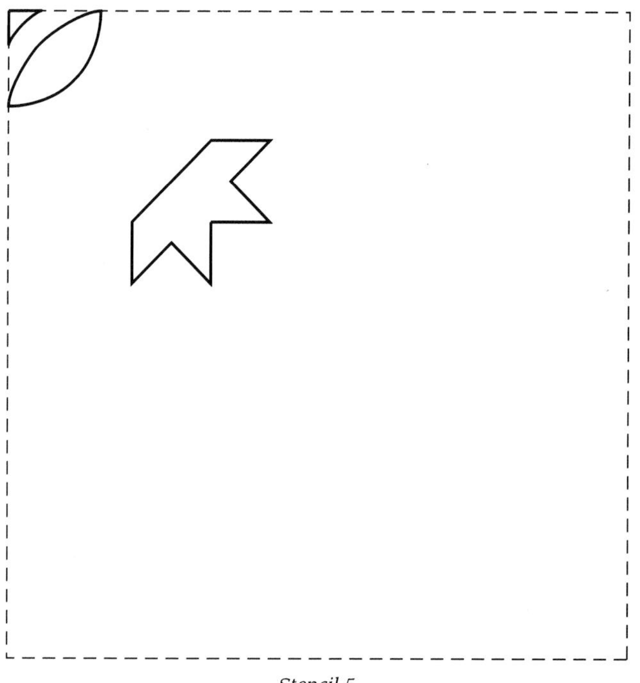

Stencil 5

17. This table is displayed in such a way that the leaf supports are easily seen. The cartoonlike features were added to the winged braces for amusement, and they do bring a smile every time a newcomer reaches eye level with the painted faces. These characters were drawn with chalk before being painted onto the painted brace. A 1-inch (2.5 cm) brush was used to squiggle in the hair, and the #4 artist's brush and 1/4-inch (6 mm) flat brush were used for everything else. See page 78 for ways to create shapes with a single brush stroke.

18. Following the same procedure you did in step 15, apply two coats of polyurethane to the table legs.

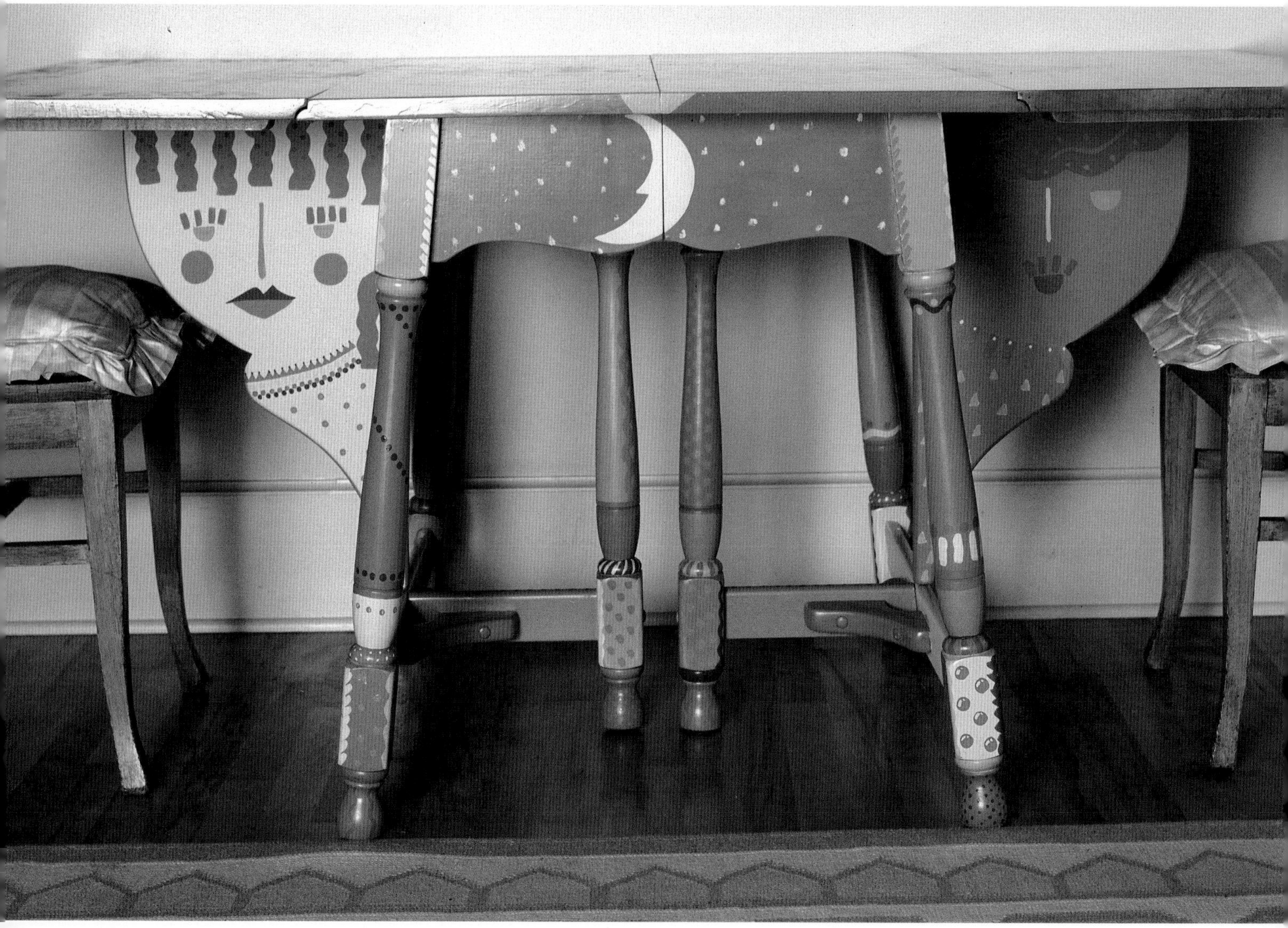

Malachite Stationery Box

Malachite is a semiprecious stone that gets its overall green color from the presence of copper. It varies in hue from a dark, greenish black to a bright, almost white, pale green (see the photograph on page 88). Its bewitching patterns of dark and light are formed by concentric lines of different widths that swirl around a central nodule. Although the patterns never repeat, they always follow the same principle.

Artisans throughout history have painted faux malachite finishes on every conceivable surface from whole rooms to tiny decorative objects. Their reproductions ranged in style from highly realistic to merely suggestive.

The faux malachite box shown here falls somewhere between the two extremes of style. Using the negative method (applying a glaze and combing some of it away), it presents a surface that is easy for the amateur to duplicate. As an exception to the general rule of selecting oil-based paint for combing, water-based paint is used here for ease and to give a softer, more natural appearance to the grain. The addition of a simulated carved ivory inlay adds interest and is very simple to make using a roller-mounted rubber stamp.

Designed to hold stationery, this box was created by connecting two discarded dresser boxes (shown below) taken from a turn-of-the-century marble-topped bureau. Such finds are always fun to work with and often free, but not always readily available. This method of reproducing malachite patterns can be applied to any project you have at hand. However, because of malachite's intense color and heavy pattern, it may be wise to start by confining your enthusiasm to smaller items such as lamp bases and jewelry boxes.

Materials

- Wooden box or other project
- White acrylic primer
- Masking tape
- Acrylic gloss varnish
- Acrylic matte varnish
- Acrylic paints: yellow, bright green, sunny yellow, and Prussian blue, white
- Adhesive cleaner

Tools

- Wet/dry sandpaper: #240, #320, and #400
- Tack cloth
- Straightedge
- #3/0 and #4/0 steel wool
- Pencil with eraser
- Craft knife
- 2 white plastic or pink rubber erasers
- 1" (2.5 cm) flat, soft bristle brush
- #2 fan blender brush
- Sheet of heavy-weight tracing vellum
- Spray bottle with fine mist adjustment
- Cotton swabs
- Paper towels
- Roller-mounted or flat rubber stamp
- Black ink pad

Instructions

1. As explained on pages 8–10, clean and prepare your project for painting. Apply two coats of acrylic primer, first across the grain, then with the grain. Allow the primer to dry well, and sand it between coats. Sanding should be very light and quick; don't sand through your base coat. Start with #240 paper, and follow with #320 and #400. Don't forget to use your tack cloth to clean the surface carefully before applying another coat of paint.

2. When your base is thoroughly dry, use tape to mask off any area where you're planning to include an ivory strip or other decoration. Use a pattern or a pencil and straightedge to mark the area first. Because of the size of my rubber stamp, I used 1-inch (2.5 cm) masking tape. After applying the tape, use a craft knife and a straightedge to trim away any excess. If you're trimming the tape where the decoration will meet the malachite or where the wood is mitered, you needn't worry about knife pressure; otherwise, use a very light hand. Next burnish the tape edges. Seal the edge of the masking tape so that paint won't leak under it by applying a coat of varnish to the entire top surface.

3. To make your malachite undercoating, mix eight parts of bright green with two parts of sunny yellow. The proportions needn't be exact, only close. You're aiming for a slightly lighter and more yellowish shade of green. Apply three or more coats of green paint to your prepared surface, painting each layer perpendicular to the last. Allow the paint to dry thoroughly, and sand between coats using #400 paper. Make sure that you have complete coverage. After allowing the paint to dry and cure for several days, lightly rub the surface with #3/0 steel wool, dust with the tack cloth, and apply a coat of matte varnish.

4. While the varnish is drying, you can make your combing tools and modify the other tools that you'll need. Two erasers should supply you with enough variations in your combing pattern. Hold each eraser on its side on a cutting surface, and slice it with a craft knife into two thin sections. The two cut pieces will have the same length and height as the original eraser, but half its original thickness. Next cut teeth into the eraser's edge, varying the spacing to make fat teeth and narrow, closely spaced teeth. (See the photograph on page 13 for an example.) Modify your fan brush by trimming 1/4 inch (6 mm) off both sides of the tip, leaving a 1/2-inch (1.3 cm) tip. Then use your craft knife to cut a 1/8-inch (3 mm) hole in the center of the eraser on your pencil.

5. Once the varnish has dried, use a pencil to draw a loose pattern of concentric curves onto one small area of the prepared surface. For guidance, refer to the close-up photograph of malachite.

6. Next, with crumpled vellum, your eraser combs, blender brush, cotton swabs, paper towels, pencil with the cut eraser, and water bottle at the ready, mix together a glaze of approximately one part Prussian blue and six parts clear gloss varnish. Using the 1-inch (2.5 cm) brush, apply the glaze over your pencil marks. Work quickly, as the glaze will dry in a matter of moments.

7. Then, with the crumpled vellum, lightly dab the entire glazed surface. Now grasp the eraser comb firmly, and hold it perpendicular to the painted surface. Starting at the edge, draw the comb along your pencil marks. Relax; it's much easier than you think. If you goof, you can always spray the surface with a little water, and wipe the glaze off with a paper towel. Remember, the idea is to enjoy yourself.

8. Once you've completed combing your pencil pattern, you need to soften some of the lines and spaces before the paint dries. Mist the surface very lightly with your spray bottle. Then place the fan brush against a line, and pull it outward until it touches the adjoining line. Continue this procedure along the entire length of the inner line, repeating it randomly at several other locations in your pattern. You may need to mist again if the glaze becomes tacky before you're finished.

9. Now dip your cotton swab in water, and dab it onto your still-wet glazed surface to form the pattern nodules. The nodules should be close together but vary in size. For a finishing touch, spray the nodules very lightly with water, dip the end of the pencil eraser into the remaining glaze, and touch the eraser to the center of each nodule. As the glaze touches the water, it will flow outward and soften.

10. After the glaze has completely dried for 24 hours, varnish the entire surface with clear acrylic gloss. Allow the surface to dry; then rub it with #4/0 steel wool, and wipe it clean with the tack cloth.

11. When the varnish is completely dry, use the craft knife and a cotton swab soaked in adhesive cleaner to ease up an edge of the masking tape. You may need to cut through the layers of varnish, glaze, and paint with a perpendicular slice along the edge of the tape to get the cleaner to soak under the tape. You risk pulling up some of the paint if you don't do this. (Should the paint come loose, replace the masking tape. Using a pointed brush, dab on a little green paint, allow it to dry, and touch up with the glaze.) Once the tape is removed, the base coat is exposed and ready to be "inlaid" with ivory.

12. Using the 1-inch (2.5 cm) brush, or a brush appropriate for your decoration, fill in the inlay area with white paint. You needn't paint a perfect edge against the malachite, but if you go over the line, wipe it off with a cotton swab. After the white paint has dried thoroughly, use a small piece of #400 paper to sand it.

13. The rubber stamp application is one step that should be practiced on paper first to figure out exactly how it works and where to start and stop. To end at the corners, place a sheet of paper at a 45-degree angle, as if you were making a miter. Once you've decided the logistics, ink your stamp, and apply the design with a firm, even stroke.

14. Any mistakes can be removed if you quickly wipe them off with a damp rag. Don't wipe too many times, though; the white paint won't take a lot of abuse.

15. When the ink is thoroughly dry, mix together ten parts of varnish and one part yellow paint. Apply this glaze quickly and smoothly to the entire surface, including the ivory. You may want to test it on a small area first to get a feel for the flow of the glaze and to make sure the color pleases you.

16. Allow the yellow glaze to dry well. Afterward, apply two coats of clear gloss varnish over the entire surface. Let the varnish dry completely between coats, rub it with #4/0 steel wool, and use the tack rag before recoating. Allow your now glorious-looking project to dry for several days, during which time you may have friends over to admire it but not to touch.

Distressed and Crackle-Glazed Welsh Cupboard

From the day I discovered antiques, I've wanted a black, antique Welsh cupboard. They're not only hard to find but also expensive. When checking with a local, unfinished furniture store, I found this inexpensive, Welsh-style cupboard, which seemed to be a good substitute.

After buying it, I discovered that there is a direct relationship between the price of a piece and the degree to which it's unfinished. I selected the furniture with the lowest price, and in so doing, I destined myself to receive a piece of furniture made of wood so rough that no amount of sanding could repair it. Additionally, as you can see in the photograph on page 94, the joints didn't fit snugly together. And, to top it all off, one front leg was wider than the other!

Do all these flaws really matter? The answer is no, not for a cupboard that should look homemade, well used, and old beyond my years. All of these imperfections enhance the final appearance of a faux antique distressed finish. (I did, however, carefully fill the joints in the molding and apply shellac to the entire surface.)

The finished black cabinet is quite handsome and at home with its prized collection of red ware. The black background, subtly broken with an intense blue crackle, heightens the drama of any display. The crackle finish isn't obvious when seen from a distance, as in the photograph opposite, but close viewing of the actual cupboard reveals this sophisticated surface treatment.

Many old cupboards were one color in an earlier era and repainted later when tastes changed. Often the base color finds its way back to the surface through wear or shows through cracks in the outer coating, gracing the furniture with a time-honored, beautiful patina. This is the surface effect that the crackle and distress techniques are designed to imitate.

Crackle isn't difficult to do but can be hard to control. Crackle medium is available at most craft stores, and the basic directions for using it can be found on the side of the bottle. I've discovered, though, that it takes a little experimentation to get just the pattern and size of crackling that's desired.

Crackle medium only works with water-based paints. The medium draws moisture out of the top coat, allowing the top coat to dry before the medium does, which causes the top coat of paint to crack. The thicker you apply the medium, the faster it draws water out of the top color. The faster the top color dries, the bigger the cracks it makes.

A beginning painter has all of the skills necessary to complete this project. It's not very complicated, and since most of the paint involved is water based, the time required from start to finish is also minimal, especially for a project this size.

Materials

- Piece of furniture
- Acrylic paints: ultra blue (8 oz/237 ml), red iron oxide (4 oz/118 ml), black (16 oz/473 ml)
- Drawer pattern enlarged to fit your project
- Tape
- Black carbon paper
- Crackle glazing medium (8 oz/237 ml)
- Small tube vermillion oil paint
- Walnut wood stain
- Satin polyurethane

Tools

- Large clean container
- 3″ (7.6 cm) flat brush
- Wet/dry sandpaper: #180, #240, #320, #400
- 2″ (5.1 cm) flat brush
- Ball-point pen with bright-colored ink
- #4 artist's round brush
- Chalk
- Awl or other pointed tool
- Rubber gloves
- Rags
- 2″ (5.1 cm) sponge applicator

Instructions

1. Before starting to paint your project, make sure that all surfaces have been cleaned, all knots shellacked, and any holes and gaps filled and sanded. See pages 8 to 10 for more information on preparing your project.

2. Instead of the usual primer for bare wood, two coats of ultra blue paint mixed with water in a four-to-one ratio are applied to the top half of the cupboard using the 3-inch (7.6 cm) brush. This is done to save both paint and time. It would take several coats of blue paint to cover white primer because this particular blue is very transparent. More importantly, though, it's done because the white primer would show when the shelves are distressed. The first coat of blue wash stains and seals the unpainted wood. It also

raises the grain, so sand the wash lightly with #400 paper, and add another layer of wash. The blue won't give even coverage, but that doesn't matter in the final finish.

3. Similarly, the lower half of the cupboard is primed in colors other than white. With the 2-inch (5.1 cm) brush, paint three coats of the red iron oxide on the door panels and drawer fronts. Sand between each coat and after the last one. When the drawer fronts are dry and smooth, tape your sized pattern into position. Slide the carbon paper underneath, carbon side down, and trace the pattern using the ball-point pen. Check to make sure that you've traced the entire silhouette before you remove the pattern and tape. Using the artist's brush, paint in the silhouette with the black paint. Repeat this procedure with the second pattern.

4. Apply three coats of black paint to the base, allowing drying time between coats. After the third coat has dried, lightly sand the painted surface with #400 paper and a little soapy water. Then apply a fourth coat of black. Allow this paint to dry and harden for one week.

5. During the week of drying time, you can do your tests for the crackle medium on a piece of scrap lumber. Paint two coats of blue in a large swath on the bare board, and allow the paint to dry. Following the manufacturer's directions, use the sponge applicator to paint the full-strength medium over a small portion of the blue swath. After the medium has dried, apply the black paint with the 2-inch (5.1 cm) brush. The cracks should start to form immediately. Once the black

paint has dried, check your crackle pattern. If you like the way it looks, then you need go no further with your tests. If you have great crevasses, then add a very small amount of water to the medium, shake it, and do another test. Proceed in this manner until you have the effect you desire.

6. Before you turn your attention to your project, you have one more tricky part to master in the art of crackle finishing. You must apply the black paint in a single pass. If you go over the black paint, it will lift and mush the medium, destroying the pattern of the crackle. Practice making straight strokes with your brush and laying the next stroke right beside the previous one, not overlapping it. For each section that you're working on, fill your brush with enough paint to complete the entire distance. It doesn't take too many tries to figure it out and master the procedure.

7. While you're waiting for the black paint to harden, you can also paint the top molding. Use the 2-inch (5.1 cm) brush to apply the red paint.

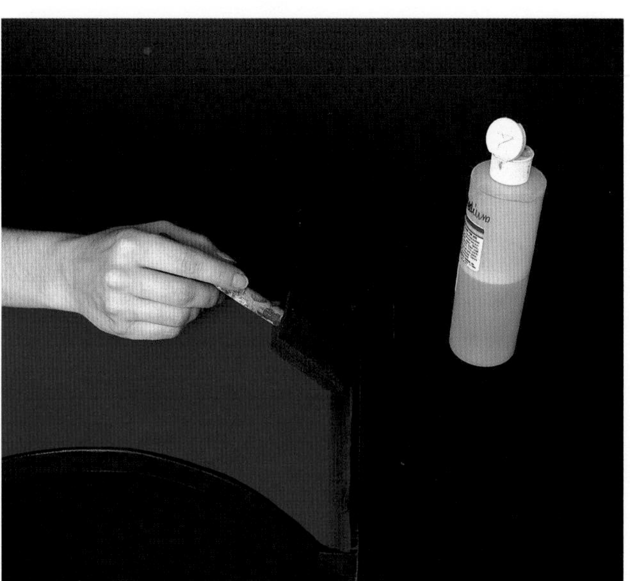

8. Before the week has elapsed, you can apply the crackle medium to the upper portion on the cupboard and complete the procedure according to your test result. I used the crackle texture on the side panels and back board of the shelf display. The subtlety of this finish wouldn't show well enough to warrant putting it on the shelves.

9. When the week has finally passed, use the chalk to mark the cupboard where you think years of wear would have eased away the paint. The edges of the shelves would become worn where pieces of china were removed and replaced night after night, year after year, decade after decade. How was the lower section used? Was bread cut there at the evening meal? Where would the master of the house have brushed against the corners of the lower section of the cupboard? Hands and fingers marked the wood when they opened the drawers and doors. Evidence of the touch of generations of people is one of the intriguing characteristics that make antiques so very unique, desirable, and irreplaceable.

10. Sand the marked areas with the #180 paper and a light but vigorous stroke. Don't sand any one area long enough to build up heat, or your water-based paint will start to stretch and roll up with the rise in temperature. Sand enough with this grade of sandpaper to remove the major portion of paint in the marked section. Then use the #240 paper briefly, then the #320, and finally the #400 to smooth the edges where the paint and the now bare wood meet. Following the same procedure, sand all of the areas that you marked with chalk. Take care not to do very much sanding on the drawer patterns or their images won't be identifiable.

11. Add a few cut marks with the awl to indicate the careless slicing of bread on the serving surface, or make some dents that tell of a change of circumstances in the cupboard's history. It might have been used as a potting bench, abused and scarred daily.

12. Wearing gloves, use a rag to apply a coat of vermillion oil-based paint directly from the tube to the newly exposed wood surfaces. Allow the vermillion to sit for 15 minutes, and wipe the excess away with a light touch. The vermillion color will show through the final stain, giving the new wood a warm glow.

13. After allowing the vermillion oil paint to cure on the wood for 30 minutes, stir the wood stain well, and apply a coat of stain to the entire cupboard. Use a clean rag to wipe off any excess. Then apply a second coat of stain to the exposed areas.

14. Allow the cupboard to dry and cure for a couple of days; then apply two coats of satin polyurethane with a clean, lint-free rag. This isn't the recommend method of application, but it gives the paint an appropriate, somewhat uneven, dull, antique finish.

Blanket Chest with a Combed Top and Painted "Hooked Rug" Panels

Being with horses is one of my greatest pleasures in life, but strangely enough, I rarely like paintings, prints, or sculptures of horses. They all appear so trite next to the real thing. Most artists seem overly possessed with the need to show a massive, powerful beast with his nostrils flared, hooves flailing, and all of his blood vessels ready to burst. That isn't the way I know horses. I know their warmth and their startling ability to communicate in a nonverbal, visual way. This is a very different animal from the one usually portrayed by artists.

That's one of the reasons why I fell in love with a picture I found of a 19th-century hooked rug showing a horse in profile. Its beauty was its simplicity. Unfortunately, when I tried to adapt the concept into a design of my own, I destroyed the very simplicity I most enjoyed. There was no valid reason to change the design in the first place, so I resolved to figure out a method for reproducing the rug in paint, complete with the hooked texture that was so appealing.

The solution that I arrived at is a technique that I've dubbed "navy-bean masking." It's a little silly and has limited applications, but so are a lot of things in life that are easy and fun.

The top of the chest is done with combed paint, which is a very old technique. It adds a rich, three-dimensional texture that provides an interesting tactile and visual treat. Combing is another technique, like vinegar painting, that evolved out of the need to produce quick imitations of wood graining. Simply explained, a comb is drawn through a layer of oil-based glaze, revealing the base color in juxtaposition with the glaze. It's necessary to use an oil glaze because water-based paint won't produce cleanly drawn impressions. This leaves the base color muddy or foggy. Also, water-based paint dries too quickly to be easily maneuvered into the correct combing pattern, and it allows for no delays or corrections. The disadvantage of the oil-based paint is the lengthy drying time, which can sometimes take up to five days.

A blanket box can be purchased at an unfinished furniture store, where you can generally find several different styles and sizes from which to choose.

Materials

- Chest or other project
- Primer of your choice (see page 10)
- 2 cans black spray enamel
- Acrylic craft paints: burnt umber, raw sienna, burnt sienna, mocha, terra cotta, old parchment (8 oz/83 ml), black, territorial beige, candy bar, palomino
- Pattern enlarged to fit your project
- White or yellow wax-free transfer paper
- 1" (2.5 cm) medium-tack masking tape (see page 15)
- 1-1/2" (3.8 cm) or 2" (5.1 cm) masking tape
- 4 bags dried navy beans (preferably small)
- Satin polyurethane
- Artist's oil paints: white, alizarin crimson, burnt sienna, vermillion hue
- Cobalt drier
- Turpentine
- Liquin

Tools

- #240 sandpaper
- Ball-point pen with bright-colored ink
- Artist's brushes: 1" (2.5 cm) and 2" (5.1 cm) flat, #2, #4, and #6 round
- Tarpaulin
- Measuring tape or ruler
- Chalk
- T-square
- Silk screening squeegee to cut for comb
- Rubber 3-sided comb, commercially available
- Craft knife or safety razor blade, with fresh cutting edge
- Pallet knife or plastic knife
- Small plastic spoon
- Clean container for mixing
- Rags

Instructions

1. Begin by making your project ready to paint. Seal any knots, prime, and sand all of the surfaces.

2. Remove the lid from the box, and take it outdoors to paint. Following all of the manufacturer's directions, spray the lid with the black paint. Allow the paint to dry and cure for five days before doing anything more to the lid. Meanwhile you can paint the base.

3. Study the picture on page 98, paying close attention to the colors, squares, and other loosely formed geometric shapes behind the horses, birds, and small tree. Keep in mind that these shapes were created originally with a needle and yarn on a canvas grid.

4. Choose a color from the paint selection, except the parchment, and begin painting freehand squares, rectangles, and other shapes on one short side of the blanket box. Change colors often, cleaning your brush with water before dipping it into another color. Butt the colors together to form a solidly painted background. Use the flat brushes for this extemporaneous paint application, keeping a freehand border of black at least 1 inch (2.5 cm) wide around the outside of the painted surface. This creates the effect of a frame. Don't worry about wet colors mushing into other wet colors; it only makes the effect more interesting.

5. When the end panel dries, repeat the procedure on all of the other sides of the box until the whole base is painted with rich browns and black.

6. When the paint has dried on all sides, position the enlarged pattern of the small tree and bird on the first end panel that you painted. Make sure that it's perfectly vertical and centered in the space. With a piece of tape placed across the top edge of the pattern, secure the pattern in position on the box. Slip a piece of transfer paper under the pattern, and trace it section by section using the ball-point pen. The bright color of the pen will allow you to know at a glance which lines have been traced and which haven't. Trace the entire tree and bird, lifting the pattern every now and then to check your progress.

7. Now paint the tree and bird with the parchment paint and the #2, #4, and #6 artist's brushes.

8. Turn the box so that a long side is facing up. Position the tree and bird pattern in the middle of the rectangle, again making sure that it's square in position. Secure it with tape. Position the pattern of the horse and bird, taping it also. Then trace everything that you have in position. When the tracing is complete, remove the horse and bird pattern, and turn it over so that the pattern faces down. If you can see the horse and bird through the paper well enough to trace it from the back side, then position, tape, and trace. If you're unable to see it well enough, then hold the copy paper over a light source (such as a window), and trace the pattern onto the back of the copy paper. Then position it on the box, tape it down, and trace it. When all the tracing is done, remove the patterns, and paint the tree, birds, and horses with the parchment paint and the #2, #4, #6, and 1-inch (2.5 cm) brushes.

9. Repeat this procedure until all four sides have been painted with their patterns.

10. Allow the paint at least a day to dry thoroughly. Then, on a perfect day, take the box outdoors to an area where you've already positioned a protective tarpaulin, and lay the box on its side with one long side facing up.

11. To paint the hooked-rug texture, you must first level the surface. Place a small handful of the navy beans in the center of the painted surface, noting which way the beans roll. Then add small stones under the tarpaulin at the corner of the box until the surface is level and the beans stop rolling off the edge.

12. Next make a "guard rail" to keep the beans from falling off the sides. Apply the 1-1/2-inch (3.8 cm) masking tape to the edges so that half of it sticks up in the air all the way around the surface.

13. Now pour the beans onto the surface, and arrange them so that they fit tightly together in a single layer with only small spaces visible between them. The spaces shouldn't be large enough to hold another bean. Walk all the way around the box to check your spacing.

14. After reading the label on the can, shake the spray paint vigorously for the length of time recommended by the manufacturer. Spray the bean-covered surface from all directions. Make sure to walk completely around again, and check for spots where the paint didn't penetrate to the lightly covered surface. Try to keep the coat of paint light, even dusty, as you spray.

15. Allow the spray paint to dry on the beans and the box for an hour. Then remove the beans, and repeat the process on the other three sides. You can use the beans over again on each of the sides. After the box has dried and cured for a few days, apply a coat of polyurethane to protect your work.

16. Measure the top of the box, and determine a size for the pattern squares that will divide equally in both directions. This box lid is painted with 5-inch (12.7 cm) squares, and it has a 1/2-inch (1.3 cm) black border on the long sides and a 3/4-inch border at the ends.

17. Mark off the squares and borders using chalk and a T-square.

18. Cut teeth into the blade of the squeegee so that it can be used to comb the paint. Mark the edge of the squeegee blade in 1/8-inch (3 mm) increments using the ball-point pen. Then cut out a 1/8-inch (3 mm) square every other space to create equal-sized teeth and gaps. You can cut teeth out of the entire blade length, or make a comb just large enough to fit your squares.

19. Apply masking tape to the right of the vertical chalk lines and around the border, and burnish the edge of the tape that is next to the chalk. The tape will make a sharp guideline between the rows of square patterns. Be sure to use medium-tack masking tape rather than the conventional type; its adhesive backing is formulated to release easily, even after a few days, without leaving a residue or damaging the paint underneath.

20. Using the plastic spoon to measure the paint, mix the glaze for the combed top. Mix together one part white, four parts alizarin crimson, two parts vermillion hue, and three parts burnt sienna. Use the pallet knife to mix all of the pigment well, leaving no streaks in the mix. Then add one part Liquin and enough turpentine to the mixture—one drip at a time—until you've mixed everything together into a thick, homogeneous liquid. Finally, stir in a spoonful of cobalt drier.

21. Combing the top is easiest if you apply the glaze to one square at a time with the 1-inch (2.5 cm) flat brush. After painting the first square, grasp the comb firmly and evenly in both hands. Align the edge of the comb with the tape, and while applying firm but light pressure with both hands equally, pull the comb through the glaze. Use the chalk or tape edge as a guide to keep the pull straight. At the end of the pull, wipe the glaze off the blade with a rag. Then set the edge of the blade along a straight guideline perpendicular to the first, and repeat the pull. This should make a checkerboard pattern. If the pattern you produce doesn't look right, paint over it with the glaze, and try again.

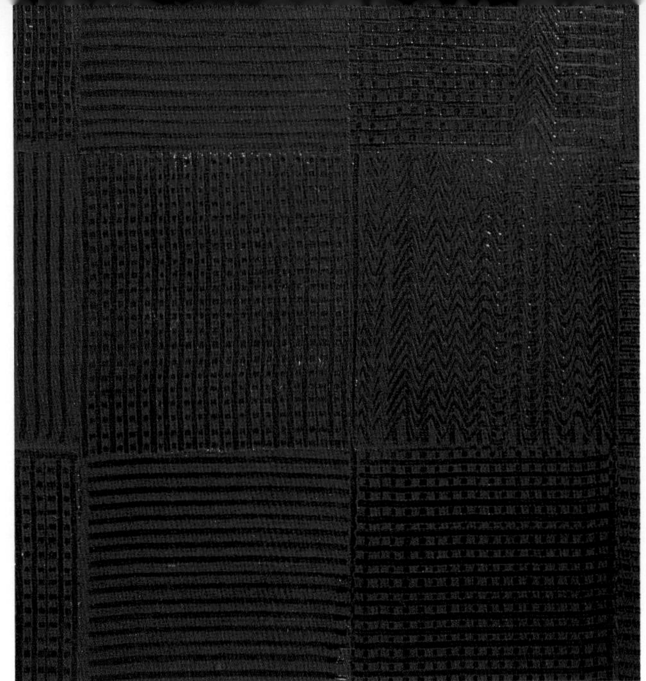

22. Complete the first row, varying the patterns from square to square. For example, pull in one direction instead of two, use the smaller triangular comb for one of the directions, and squiggle the comb back and forth as it travels through the glaze. Establish a few different patterns, and stick with them for the entire top. Don't place the same patterns next to one another or you will lose the overall square pattern. After you've completed the first row of combing, remove the tape, pulling it carefully away from the wet glaze. Continue with each row until the entire top is complete.

23. Set the lid aside to dry for at least 10 days. You can check to make sure the paint is hard by pressing on it with your fingernail. If it doesn't dent easily, it's dry. A final coat of polyurethane, applied with the 2-inch (5.1 cm) brush, is recommended if the top will be subject to wear.

Men's Plaid Chest

Tall and handsome, with a touch of roughness in the plaid, this well-groomed chest provides perfect storage for a man's clothing. It's lean form and the businesslike attitude of its masculine geometric pattern should fit comfortably in almost any bedroom.

This project is designed for the painter who likes the look of straight lines and geometric shapes but has a phobia when it comes to small brushes and tightly controlled work. Watercolor pencils give a tailored, well dressed effect to this plaid cabinet without making you suffer through the frustration of trying to paint a sharp-edged, perfectly straight line. Masking tape, a straightedge, and watercolor pencils make all of those problems a thing of the past.

A project this size requires approximately 40 hours of work from start to finish. This may sound like a long time, but the work itself is undemanding and can easily be done in small segments of time and with frequent interruptions. The mess associated with paint is present only in the first few hours of the project, so work space is flexible, too.

In addition to decorating a dresser, this plaid has many possible applications. It could be reproduced on a trunk for a stunning transformation; the coffee table in the family room could take on a whole new personality with a few lines of a tartan plaid; even a small box could become a scene stealer with a little Scottish plaid trim.

Materials

- Furniture or other wooden project
- Primer of your choice (see page 10)
- Hunter green interior/exterior, acrylic matte latex enamel
- Deep magenta interior/exterior, acrylic semigloss enamel
- Grid paper
- Masking tape
- Watercolor pencils: white, light blue, raspberry, turquoise, golden yellow
- Cotton swabs
- Matte spray fixative
- White acrylic craft paint
- Water-based matte polyurethane

Tools

- 2" (5.1 cm) foam applicator
- #400 wet/dry sandpaper
- Long straightedge
- Pencil sharpener
- Cotton swabs

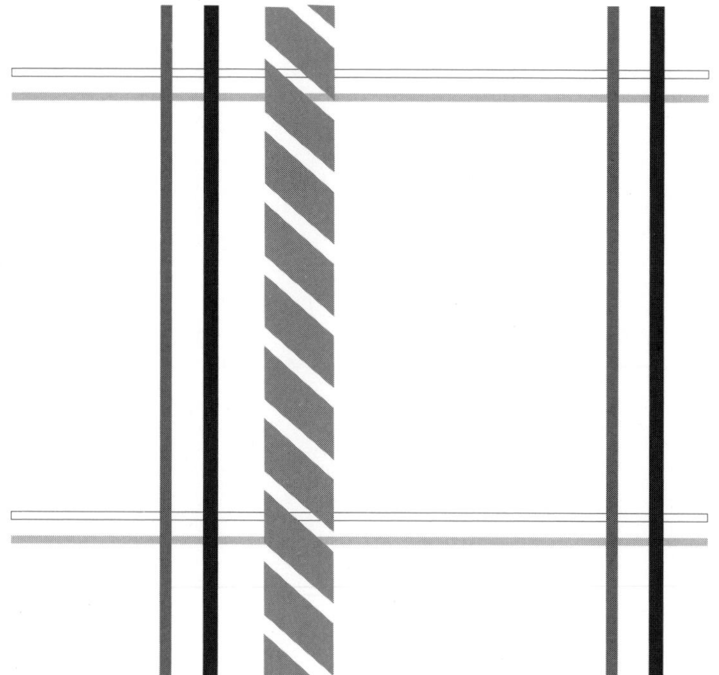

Instructions

1. This piece of unfinished furniture had to be checked over thoroughly before the project was begun. The fit of the drawers and doors had to be square, even, and flush. Drawer runners had to be adjusted to make the drawers parallel when closed. Other defects had to be corrected as much as possible. Choosing more expensive furniture may have eliminated many of these flaws, so the amount of cash you want to invest versus the level of frustration you are willing to bear is a definite consideration.

Before starting to paint, remove the hardware, and fill any flaws in your project. Then prime the wood, and finely sand the surface.

2. Apply a coat of slightly thinned green paint to the body of the cabinet with the foam applicator. Once the paint has dried thoroughly, lightly sand it with the #400 paper and a little soapy water. For each of two additional coats of paint, allow the paint to be a little thicker, but make sure that it still flows on with ease. Apply each coat perpendicular to the previous one to avoid leaving applicator marks, and wet-sand between coats with the #400 paper. Your base coat must have a smooth surface for you to do your pencil work.

3. Using the applicator and the deep magenta paint, paint the top molding, door and drawer pulls, dresser base, and legs.

4. Use the grid paper to develop your own plaid, copying one from a piece of fabric or reproducing the one used here.

5. Figure out where you want the plaid to fall on the piece of furniture. Do you want it perfectly centered or a little off-center for a more interesting arrangement? Will all of the vertical and horizontal lines fall in trouble-free areas, or will your geometric precision be disturbed by a piece of troublesome molding? Adjust the position of your plaid grid until you've solved all of these problems. It's much easier than it sounds, but keep in mind that the smaller the plaid, the more work and complications involved.

6. Once you've decided upon the location of each of the lines in your plaid, tape the pattern grid into position at the top of the section or series of drawers where you want to start. Then use watercolor pencils (in the correct colors) to mark the right and left edges of each of the vertical lines. After you've marked all the verticals at the top, move the grid to the bottom of your work area, and mark the corresponding bottoms of the vertical lines. Make sure that you align the verticals at top and bottom. Then use the straightedge and the watercolor pencils, sharply pointed, to connect the marks with a clearly drawn line. It's wise to step back from your work after you make the first lines, just to be sure that everything looks straight and square. Don't make the lines for the broad blue stripe the same way you do the others; instead, draw these lines very lightly and intermittently.

7. Use the masking tape to connect the marks from top to bottom for the bright blue stripe, burnishing down the inside edges of the tape. Use the light blue pencil to color 1/4-inch (6 mm) diagonal bands of blue along the length of the stripe, leaving a 1/8-inch (3 mm) break between the blue bands. If the intermittent vertical line falls in the wrong place, erase it with a slightly damp cotton swab.

8. Color in the other vertical stripes with the appropriate pencils, sharpening them often to keep your work crisp. If you go outside the guide lines, use a dampened cotton swab and the straightedge as a guide. Rub the swab back and forth along the straightedge to remove only the unwanted pencil. Finish all the vertical lines before starting the horizontal ones, making sure to extend the lines along the edges of drawers and doors to match them up with the continuing lines on the base cabinet.

9. Now position the pattern grid at the top of your project, lining up the grid with the lines already drawn. Tack the grid paper in position with masking tape, and mark all the horizontal stripes the same way that you did the vertical ones, working from left to right instead of from top to bottom. Connect all the marks with the sharpened watercolor pencil, and color in the stripes.

10. When all of the plaid on one side of the cabinet is finished, spray your work with matte fixative. Then turn the piece so that another side faces up, and continue penciling in the plaid, following the same steps. Don't forget to mist each area with fixative as you complete it to protect it from damp fingers and other hazards. Be sure to spray the fixative lightly, building up a protective coat in successive dry layers; otherwise, your watercolor pencil may run. The fixative has quite a strong odor, so it's best to use it outdoors and avoid facing the wrath of your family.

11. Once the entire cabinet has been covered with plaid, you can dress up the drawer pulls by dotting white paint over the deep magenta base color, making a pattern similar to that of a pin-dot tie.

12. Finish the cabinet with two coats of matte polyurethane to seal and preserve the pencil marks. Then reassemble all of the parts.

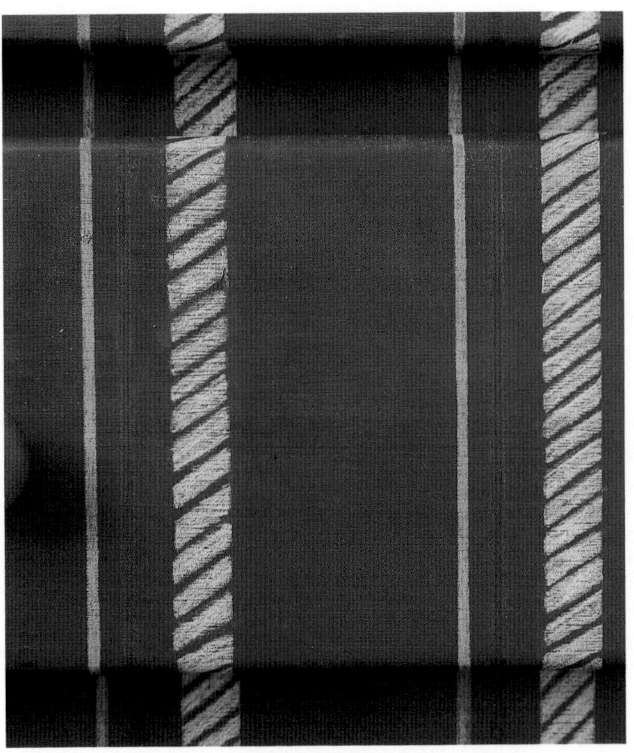

Hunt Scene on a Wooden Lamp Base

This is a great project for those who have never painted a picture in their lives, not even in kindergarten. You don't believe me, I can tell. Take a quick look at the close-up photographs of the work in progress, and you'll lose a little of your skepticism. After reading the instructions, you may decide that you could do some parts but that others look too difficult. My advice is to try everything on a scrap piece of board. Just follow the instructions, relax, and above all, don't aim for perfection, or you'll destroy the character in your work that makes it uniquely yours. I'm willing to bet that you'll love the results.

The pattern of this bucolic scene is designed to fit an armoire or a lamp, no matter what the width or height. The pattern wraps all the way around the lamp, showing a red brick house on the other side, so you have plenty of room to adjust for the proportions you need. If, for instance, you were painting the front of a cabinet that is 5 feet (1.5 m) wide and 6 feet (1.8 m) tall, you would use the entire front panel and most of both side panels of the pattern.

Additionally, you could change the houses to resemble your own. The gray frame home shown in the photograph opposite is the house where we live now, and the red brick house is an adaptation of the one where I grew up. The proportions aren't accurate, but that's unimportant. These somewhat primitive renderings are meant to be purely decorative and unsophisticated in the manner of folk art. The shading and shadows aren't necessary, and you may choose not to include them in your work.

Materials

- 6" x 14" x 3-1/2" (15.2 x 35.6 x 8.9 cm) block of wood
- 2 decorative wood panels (see below)
- Lamp kit
- Gesso
- Pattern sized to fit
- Masking tape
- Acrylic craft paints: white, pale blue, old parchment, medium gray, rainforest green, holly green, green sea, bluegrass green, black, red, red iron oxide, burnt sienna, palomino
- White fine-line paint pen
- Black extra-fine waterproof marker
- Matte water-based polyurethane
- Red mahogany wood stain, small amount
- Gloss polyurethane, small amount

Tools

- Drill with 7/16" (1.1 cm) extra-long bit or bit extension
- Fine sandpaper
- Black carbon paper
- Ball-point pen with bright-colored ink
- 2 - #4 tapered point brushes, 1 trimmed into scumble brush (see below)
- 7 clean containers with lids
- Permanent marker
- Measuring spoons

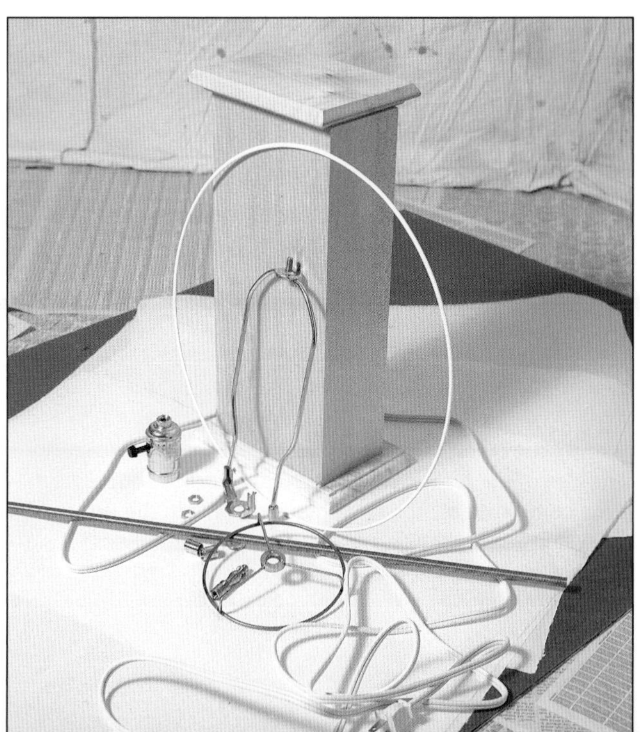

Instructions

1. First assemble all of your materials and tools. If you want to make a lamp just like this one, you should purchase a kit that contains the hoop, threaded rod, light socket with switch, finial, electrical cord and plug, and the rest of the hardware necessary to assemble a lamp. The wooden block for the base must be drilled *straight* through the center, from top to bottom, with a 7/16-inch (1.1 cm) hole. You can find the unfinished decorative wood panels for the top and bottom of your base at a craft store; they're designed to be used as the bases for brass plaques. Drill these panels through their centers with the same 7/16-inch (1.1 cm) hole. Prime the wood block with gesso, and sand it lightly.

2. To make your scumble brush, trim an old and well used or an inexpensive #4 brush with a sharp safety razor blade, making a blunt cut and leaving the bristles about 1/2 inch (1.3 cm) long. Place the brush flat on a cutting board to perform this operation. You don't have to sacrifice one of your sable brushes for this project; squirrel will do fine as long as the brush has some spring and life left in it.

3. Position the pattern on the wood block or other piece of furniture, making sure that the pattern fits or that you've made all of the necessary adjustments to the size of the pattern. Tape the pattern to the block at the top, using the tape as if it were a hinge so that you can flip the pattern back and forth as you alternate tracing and painting.

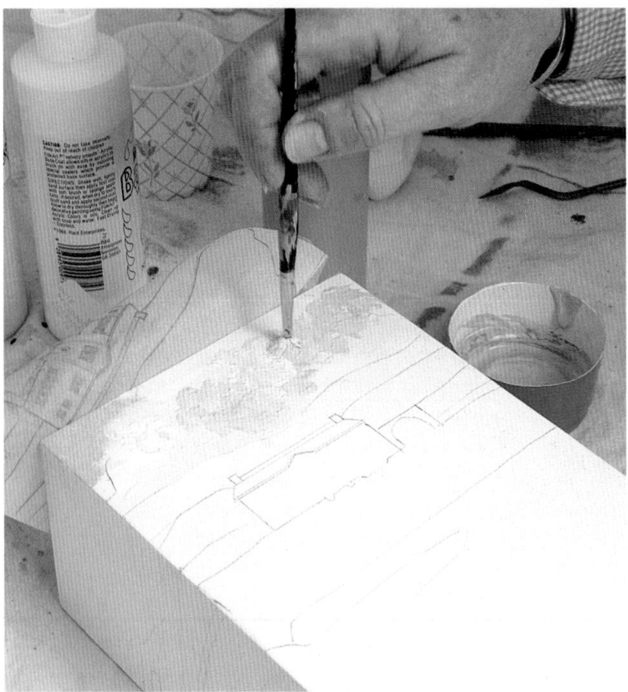

4. Insert the carbon paper face down, and begin transferring the image with the ball-point pen. For now, trace only the outline of the hills and the house. Don't trace the fences, horses, riders, or house details; trace just the base sections of color. Check your work, and flip the pattern out of the way, but don't remove the tape.

5. Mix together the blue paint with some white to get an ice blue, adding a few drops of water to thin the paint. Mix together a little white paint with the parchment. Have on hand some clean water to wash your brush. For the brush, use the trimmed #4 scumble brush. Place a blob of the ice-blue paint in each of the upper corners; then clean your brush. Dip the brush into the lightened parchment, dabbing it into the center of the sky. After cleaning it again, dip the brush into the white paint. Dab the white into the parchment sky with an up and down motion, mashing the brush a bit as you go. Mash one color into another, but don't blend them well. Let them make their own intermediate colors and find their own places in the sky.

6. Paint the body of the house, without any details, with the red iron oxide. It's not important to paint sharp edges where two colors come together because you will define those edges later.

7. Next paint the mountains, hills, and sections of the lawn with seven shades of green. Mix the seven shades of green paint using the formulas below, starting with a light gray that has just a slight bit of green color to it and progressing through an almost black shade of green. The proportions given are for this lamp base. If you're making a larger project, the quantities of paint must be increased proportionally. Before you begin to mix the colors, number your storage containers with the permanent marker.

#1: 1 teaspoon (5 ml) white and 2 teaspoons (10 ml) rain-forest green.

#2: 1 teaspoon (5 ml) each of white, rain-forest green, and green sea.

#3: 4 teaspoons (20 ml) green sea and 1/2 teaspoon (2.5 ml) rain-forest green.

#4: 1 teaspoon (5 ml) white, 4 teaspoons (20 ml) rain-forest, and 1/2 teaspoon (2.5 ml) bluegrass.

#5: 2 teaspoons (10 ml) green sea, 2 teaspoons (10 ml) holly green, and 1/2 teaspoon (2.5 ml) black.

#6: 3 teaspoons (15 ml) green sea, 9 teaspoons (45 ml) holly green, and 3 teaspoons (15 ml) black.

#7: 1 teaspoon (5 ml) green sea, 3 teaspoons (15 ml) holly green, and 2 teaspoons (10 ml) black.

All of these mixtures should be kept tightly covered until they're used. You'll need them on all four sides of the lamp.

8. Start painting with green #1. This shade of green is used on the line of mountains next to the sky. The row of hills a little farther forward is painted with green #2. The pasture, the block of space below the hills and adjacent to the sides of the house, is painted with green #3. Green #4 is the color used for the lawn that's directly in the front of the house and extends all the way to the first horizontal line. Use green #5 for the small wedge shape that butts the horizontal lower line of green #4 and extends about

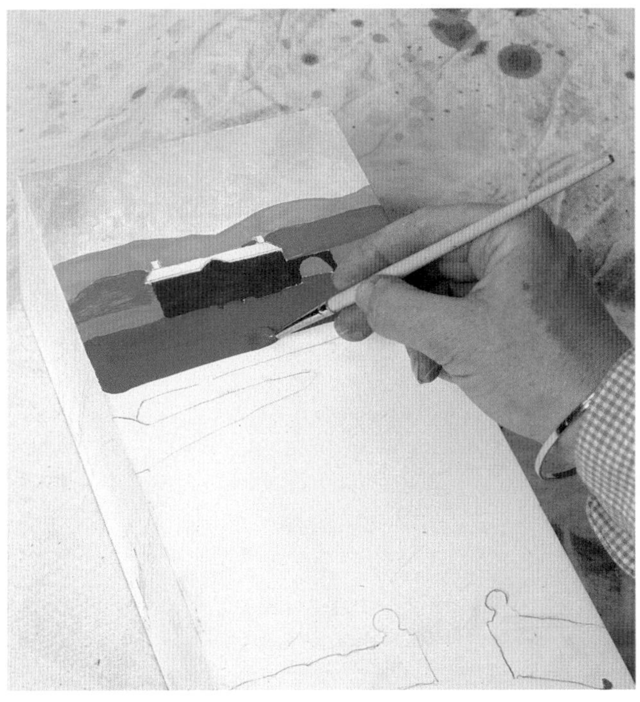

halfway across the front panel. Paint the rest of the foreground except for the stone wall with green #6.

9. Paint the background of the stone wall and the roof of the house with the medium gray.

10. When the paint is dry, flip the pattern and carbon paper back into tracing position. Use the ball-point pen to transfer the outline of the evergreens, the shrubs around the house and in the foreground, and the trees and their trunks in the back pasture and hills. Then flip the pattern back out of the way.

11. Use a little green sea and the scumble brush to dab in the tops of the trees. Barely dip the tip of the good #4 brush into green #7, and paint in the trunks of the trees by lightly stroking straight down for about 1/8 to 1/4 inch (3 to 6 mm) under the center of the tree tops.

12. Continue using the good #4 brush to paint the evergreens and shrubs with green #7. To suggest sunlight, water down a very small amount of green #3, and apply it on the tops of the shrubs. Use just the tip of the brush to apply the highlights.

13. When the paint is dry, return the pattern to its tracing position. Trace the details on the house except for the detail in the windows, the fences, the horses and riders, the dogs, and the stones of the wall. Flip the pattern back away from your work.

14. Use the #4 brush, tip only, and the light blue paint to dot in the windows of the house. Don't worry about filling the whole space with blue; a suggestion of color will work. Dot in a little white too.

15. Following the manufacturer's directions, use the white paint pen to draw the fence. Draw short lines to make up one solid line. Do the horizontal rails first, then the fence posts. Use the pen also to draw the line that indicates the roof overhang (between the bricks and the roof).

16. Paint the stones on the wall with the palomino paint and your untrimmed #4 brush. With the same brush, paint the riders' boots and hats in black. Then paint the riders' jackets in red.

17. Paint the horses in blacks, browns, white, and—of course—palomino. You may want to paint the horses in their entirety all at one time. Then replace the pattern, and trace the riders' legs and horse details.

18. Paint the dogs in white, and add their black spots.

19. Use the fine-line marker, or reposition the tracing paper, and trace the horse bridles, hooves, and dogs' eyes onto the surface with the carbon paper.

20. Using the brown, paint the door to the house and the porch. Return the pattern to the tracing position, and trace the house details in the windows, door, steps, roof outline, railings, and vertical lines that define the bay windows and other architectural details. You may want to use a straight-edge when tracing the railing and house outline because you won't be painting over the black carbon lines.

21. To give shadow and depth to your painting, use your scumble brush and green #7. Work with the brush almost dry. Dip the end of the brush in the paint, and work off most of the color onto a piece of scrap paper. Lightly tamp in shadows under the horses and dogs and, if you like, add a little texture to the lawn by tamping in the dark green off to the right or left side of the picture. Be sparing, and keep your brush fairly dry. If the paint appears too dark, thin it with a little water, and continue tamping it on with the dry brush.

22. Add the suggestion of walkways the same way that you added the shadows, but use the palomino paint and an even drier brush. Tamp on a little palomino where you would find a drive, a passage through the stone wall, and a walkway in front of the house. Use the good brush to dot specks of palomino around the fountain.

23. Following the same general instructions, complete the other three sides of the lamp.

24. Stain the wood panels for the top and bottom of the lamp, and apply two coats of gloss polyurethane. Apply a coat of matte polyurethane to the body of the lamp. When the finish is dry, assemble the lamp parts according to the directions supplied with the lamp assembly kit.

25. To purchase a color-coordinated shade, take the base with you to your local lamp shop. Alternatively, I recommend a plain black shade.

Faux Oriental Lacquer Table

True Oriental lacquer finishes, which first appeared in China around the middle of the 15th century, are something to be viewed with reverence. Because of their depth and subtlety, these finishes can be truly appreciated only in three-dimensional form. Up to 100 coats of lac, the sap from the Rhus vernicifera, a tree native to China, are applied to a piece of furniture. The lac is dried slowly in damp conditions, building up the surface to a luster more like that of polished stone than anything manmade.

As the demand for Oriental lacquer increased, the methods for creating the finish became more streamlined. In the 17th century, European craftsmen created a process using multiple layers of shellac to produce a deep, glossy surface that somewhat resembled Oriental lacquer. This method was much quicker and required fewer varnish coats than true lacquer, but it still demanded careful drying under a protective tent to ensure a smooth, blemish-free surface. The shellac process was called japanning, a term designed to cash in on the appeal of the exotic Oriental lacquer furnishings.

Making a faux lacquer finish today does take time and patience, but not a lifetime. The underlying red paint is oil based, but fast-drying polyurethane is used to replace the traditional lac and shellac. You may determine for yourself the number of coats of varnish that you apply to your project. If you're the least bit serious, it will be more than four, but far fewer than 100. The result is a perfect-looking finish that makes a handsome display piece.

In place of a protective tent, you can use a bath or shower enclosure. With the door closed or curtain pulled, this will provide a relatively dust-free environment for drying your faux lacquer. Since you're using polyurethane in place of natural lac, you won't require moist air to achieve a smooth finish.

The proportions of this table are charming, and its simplicity of line is in keeping with the traditional ascetic nature of Oriental lacquer work. Oriental craftsmen considered the finish alone to be embellishment enough. The trompe l'oeil marbles are a break with that custom, but so is the method of producing the finish. I've long been captivated by the sometimes gaudy beauty of marbles with their garish colors locked beneath the flawless surface of the glass. Somehow I connect marbles with the surface of a lacquered table that only mellows with time.

For this project, choose a piece of furniture with smooth wood, one that doesn't have heavy, obvious wood graining. Coarse grain, such as oak, will make getting the perfect wood finish too much work. Choose a piece that is also simple in design, with little or no ornamentation.

Materials

- Wooden furniture project
- White shellac
- Red oil-based flat enamel
- Gesso
- Cotton swabs
- Small quantity of acrylic craft paint in your choice of colors, plus black and white
- 1-1/2" (3.8 cm) wood ball
- Double-ended wood screw
- Artist's oil paints: your choice of colors for the marbles, plus black
- Cobalt drier
- Linseed oil
- Turpentine
- Mineral spirits
- Semigloss polyurethane
- Gloss polyurethane

Tools

- Wet/dry sandpaper: #240, #320, #400
- Brushes: shellac brush, 1/2" (1.3 cm) and 2" (5.1 cm) best quality flat, #2 and #4 round, #6 badger blender with plastic sleeve
- Piece of paper
- Pencil
- Circle guide
- Scissors
- Fine-line white paint pen
- Pallet knife
- Clean, shallow containers
- Enclosed shower stall or tub large enough to hold your project
- Shims
- Level

Instructions

1. Sand the table well, and fill and sand all flaws in the surface until they're perfectly smooth. Sand off any of the sharp edges to prevent the edges from sanding through too easily later. Then find a level working surface where the paint layers can dry undisturbed.

2. The white shellac primer needs to be silky smooth because any flaws in the primer will sing through all of the following layers. Use your shellac brush to apply the first coat of primer across the grain. Apply the second coat perpendicular to the first. Wet-sand between coats with #320 paper, and wet-sand the second coat with #320 and #400 papers. Make sure that there are no paint ridges or flaws before continuing with the red paint. You may need a third coat of primer. For more information on white shellac, see page 10.

3. Apply the red paint with the 2-inch (5.1 cm) brush. Start with a coat of red slightly thinned with mineral spirits, and follow the same procedure as you did with the primer application, changing directions with each layer. Allow the paint to be slightly thicker, but still smoothly flowing, with each coat. You need to apply at least four coats of red paint, sanding with #400 paper and a little soapy water between each coat. There are seven coats of red on this table. Be sure to wipe the table with a damp cloth to make it free of dust each time before applying paint. Wet-sand the top coat of paint with the #400 paper.

4. Start the marbles by first drawing circles on a piece of paper the actual size of real marbles: 5/8 inch (1.6 cm), 7/8 inch (2.2 cm), and 1 inch (2.5 cm). If you have a large table top, you may even want 2-inch (5.1 cm) "boulders." Use the pencil and circle guide to draw the marbles on a piece of paper, and cut out the circles along the pencil lines. Place the circles of paper on the painted table top, and move them around until they look as though they're positioned naturally. You can use real marbles to help you determine the placement. If you have real marbles for this process, place them gently on the table and light them strongly from one direction, observing their shadows and reserving the visual memory for later use.

5. Using a pencil, lightly mark the spots that you've chosen for the marbles. Then use the circle guide and pencil to draw the marble shapes on the table. Draw the shadow of the marble with a slightly smaller circle placed behind the larger one. Make sure that all of the shadows are offset at the same angle from the marbles.

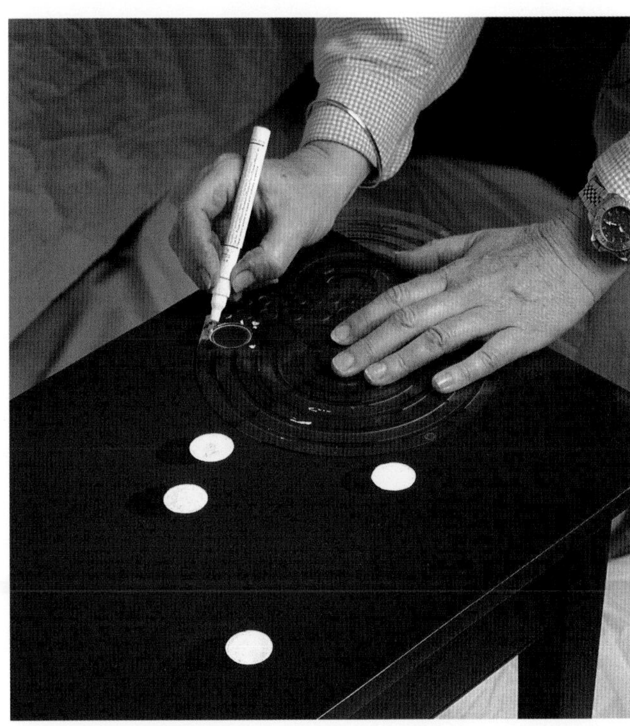

6. Letting the pencil line be the outside border, paint the shadows in black or charcoal grey with the #4 brush. Don't go over the pencil line.

7. Now use the paint pen and the circle guide to outline the marbles directly over the pencil marks. Paint the

circles with the gesso and #4 brush, painting over as much of the line of the paint pen as you can without going outside the circle.

8. When the gesso dries, you're ready to paint the marbles. The trick to getting a marbled effect is to apply water-based paint over oil paint while the oil paint is still wet, and vice versa. It doesn't matter whether you start with a water- or oil-based paint, only that you apply the opposite medium to the still-wet base color for each layer. Plan and prepare all of your colors for each marble in advance. Mix the oil colors with a drop of drier and some mineral spirits until they flow without much resistance.

9. Using the #4 brush, paint the first marble with yellow water-based paint. The entire interior needn't be covered.

10. Use the #2 brush and the thinned red oil-based paint to trail a line of color through the wet yellow paint. The wet water-based paint resists the oil paint, causing some interesting effects.

11. Green water-based paint is added next with the aid of the #2 brush. The yellow and green paint may flow together and create a third color, enhancing the overall effect.

12. Apply black paint with the #4 brush to fill in the blanks. When the paint is dry, place a white highlight on the marble to reflect the light source that created the shadows. A cotton swab is used to create this image because it gives a soft, realistic reflection.

13. When you're sure that all of the paint is completely hard and dry—after at least a few days of drying time—arrange the set-up for allowing the varnished table to dry in your shower or bath enclosure. Place the level on top of the table, and use shims or pieces of wood under the legs to establish a perfectly level plane for the table to sit on while the coats of varnish are drying. You may find all this very tricky when you have to work around the family's bathing schedule. Whenever I have a piece drying in the tub, I hang a red ribbon over the shower curtain rod so that no one will turn on the water and ruin a wet finish or, worse yet, fall into a piece of furniture sitting where it doesn't really belong.

14. Apply a layer of gloss polyurethane with the 2-inch (5.1 cm) brush. The polyurethane for this first coat should be thinned with mineral spirits on a five-to-one ratio. Apply it gingerly to the table top, without going over the varnish once you've made one pass. You don't want to disturb the paint at the edge of the circles left there by the paint pen. You can varnish the base of the table while you're waiting for the marbles to dry. Watch carefully for drips. Set the table in the enclosure, and let the polyurethane dry. Very lightly sand the dried polyurethane with the #400 paper, applying just enough pressure to remove the brush hairs and dust and to prepare the surface for the next coat of paint.

15. Now mix the glaze. Squeeze about 1/8 inch (3 mm) from the tube of black paint into a clean, shallow container, and use the pallet knife to mix in a few drops of linseed oil. Add the oil a drop at a time until you've blended in a total of five drops. Using the same method, mix in three drops of drier and an equal amount of turpentine.

16. Apply a stroke of paint to the corners of the table with the 1/2-inch (1.3 cm) brush. Then place the plastic sleeve of your badger blender brush so that it covers all but about 1/4 inch (6 mm) of the bristles. With a very light up-and-down motion, tamp the dry badger brush into the edge of the black paint, gradually tamping the paint to an ever fainter amount as you work toward the center of the top, drawer front, or table apron. This creates a halo effect. Allow a solid stripe of paint to fill any decorative depressions. You can also add a little of this shading at the top of each of the legs. Allow the glaze to dry in your dust-free bath enclosure.

17. The faux marble drawer pull made from a wooden ball fools anyone who sees it for the first time. This is probably due to its very shiny finish. Prime the ball with gesso, and apply the paint using the same procedure as you followed for the marbles on the table top. The only difference here is that dabs of paint, as opposed to trails of color, are used to make the marble's pattern. Attach the double ended wood screw to the ball before starting to paint. This will allow the ball to be screwed into a scrap piece of wood, eliminating finger prints and drying position problems. Let the paint on the ball dry and cure for 10 days before applying multiple coats of gloss polyurethane.

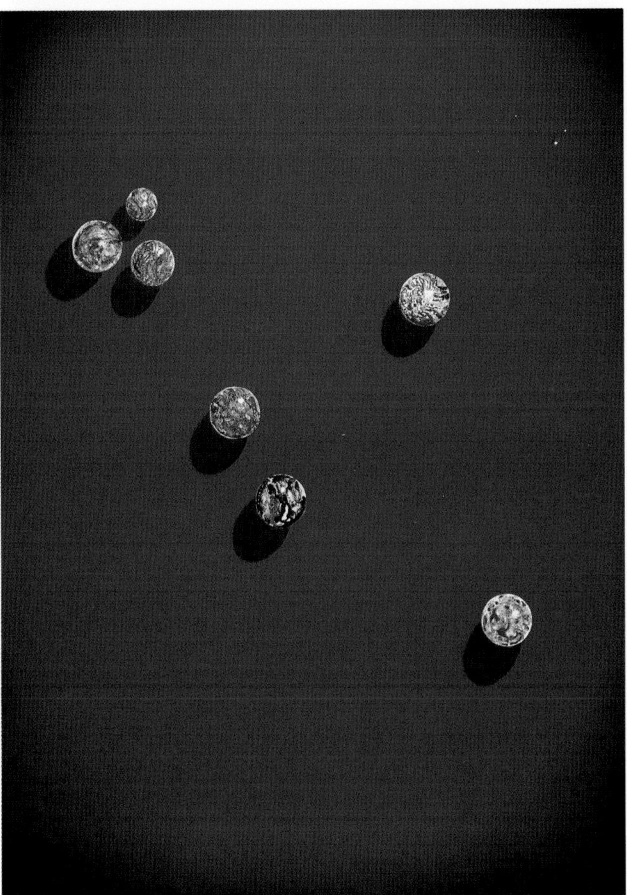

18. Now is the time for the coup de grâce. Using a small amount of the glossy polyurethane, mix five parts of polyurethane with one part mineral spirits. Apply this mixture to the dust-free table with the 2-inch (5.1 cm) brush, allow it to dry in the bath stall, and lightly wet-sand the finish with the #400 paper until there are no flaws such as brush bristles, hair, or dust. Apply a second coat of glossy polyurethane that has been thinned with mineral spirits on an 8:1 ratio. Apply each additional coat perpendicular to the last, and reduce the amount of mineral spirits until you're using the polyurethane right out of the can. Repeat the drying and wet-sanding procedure; then apply a coat of *semi*-gloss polyurethane thinned 10:1 with spirits. Continue to apply the semigloss polyurethane until you cry "uncle." Then apply one more coat to the table top.

19. Finish the faux marble drawer pull in the same manner as you did the table, but use only the gloss polyurethane for all of the layers of varnish.

Footstool with Feet Painted to Match Fabric

Looking as sweet as a cake, this fat little footstool isn't just a painting project; it's also a stool built from scratch, just like any good cake. A piece of foam rubber is glued to a thick piece of plywood, then covered in fabric, and mounted on three ball-shaped fence finials that have been painted to match the fabric. With some fringe and other trims added, the result shown is a rather Victorian looking footstool. Choose a different fabric, and the final product could be any style: a southwest print trimmed with braid or beadwork, a contemporary geometric with polka dot feet, or a green tartan plaid with red trim.

No matter what your choice of style, the procedure is the same, and the painting on the feet can be as simple as you like for a very successful result. I got a little more carried away with these feet than I had intended. My plan was simply to apply dabs and dots of paint in colors matching the fabric, and this is the approach I recommend. However, if you want to get as carried away as I did, here's an example of what "carried away" looks like.

The materials and tools needed for this project are easy to find if you don't already have them. You'll need only basic woodworking tools and skills (cutting and drilling), and you won't need a sewing machine to complete the project. The materials are shown in the photograph below.

Materials

- 17" (43.2 cm) square of 1"-thick (2.5 cm) plywood*
- Masking tape
- 3 blocks of wood, each 1" x 2" x 3" (2.5 x 5.1 x 7.6 cm)
- Wood glue
- 3 round or acorn-shaped fence-post tops
- 8" x 17" dia. (20.3 x 43.2 cm) disk of foam rubber or 2 - 4" (10.2 cm) disks hot-glued together
- Upholstery or nylon twine
- Acrylic craft paints to match your fabric
- Fabric measuring 60" x 24" (152.4 x 61 cm)
- 60" (152.4 cm) of 2" (5.1 cm) trim, fringe, or ruffle
- Optional additional trim (cording, etc.)
- 5" x 3/8" (12.7 x 1 cm) dowel rod
- 2" (5.1 cm) button

*Make sure that your plywood has straight edges and that all corners are 90°.

Tools

- Straightedge with hole at one end
- Measuring tape or ruler
- Pencil
- Ball-point pen
- Saber saw
- Drill with bit same size as double-ended wood screws on fence-post tops
- Cool-melt glue gun and several glue sticks
- Spring clamp
- 5" (12.7 cm) or longer craft needle
- Scissors
- 1/2" (1.3 cm) flat artist's brush
- #4 round artist's brush
- Staple gun

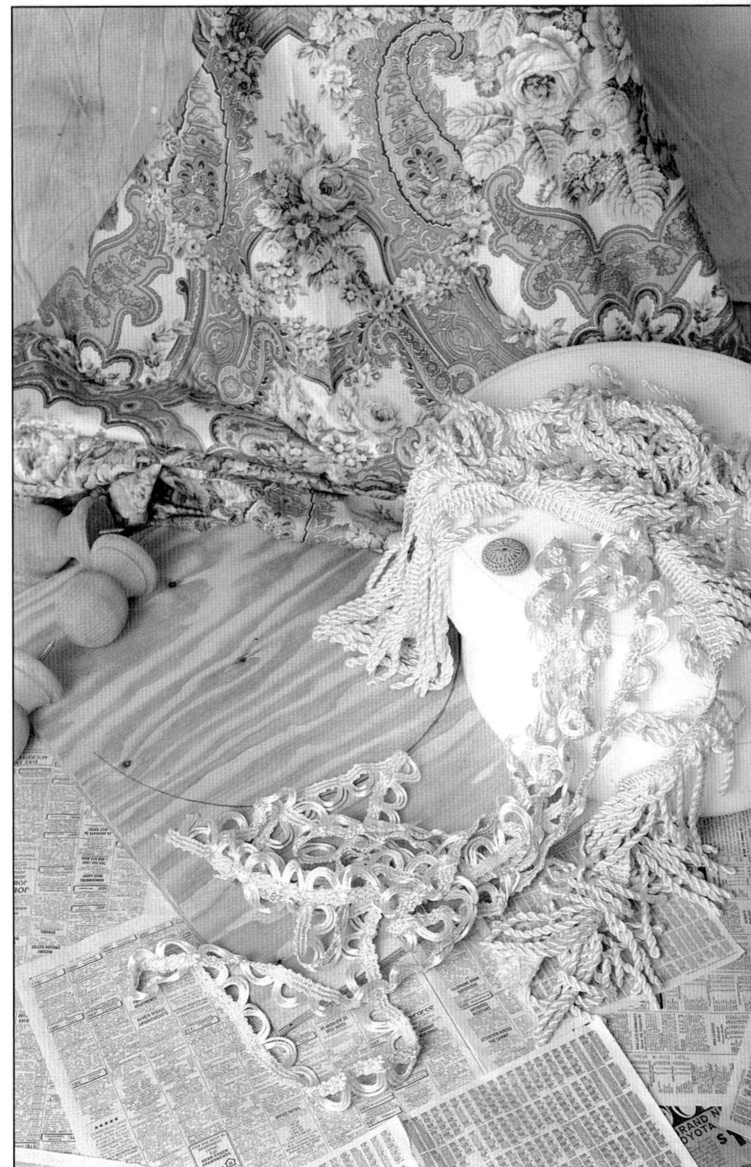

Instructions

1. To draw a large circle on a piece of plywood, measure from the center of the hole at the end of your straightedge to a point 8-1/2" (21.6 cm) away, and tape your sharpened pencil to the side of the straightedge at this spot. The pencil point should extend about 1 inch (2.5 cm) from the back side of the straightedge. I sliced a notch out of the pencil so that the pencil would slide onto the edge of my straightedge, making it easier to hold in position.

2. If your plywood is exactly 17 inches (43.2 cm) square, measure 8-1/2 inches (21.6 cm) in from two perpendicular edges of the plywood. Mark this point, which will be the center of the circle, by making a depression with the tip of the ball-point pen. Insert the end of the pen through the hole at the end of the straightedge and into the dent created by the pen point. If you're right handed, hold the pen in your left hand, and use your other hand to hold the pencil and draw the circle.

If your plywood is larger than 17 inches (43.2 cm) square, you may wish to position your circle away from the edges so that you have more leeway when cutting it. Once you've drawn your circle, use your straightedge to draw a 17-inch (43.2 cm) square with its sides just touching the edges of the circle.

3. Before you cut the plywood circle, draw an equilateral triangle with its points touching the circle. To do this, mark a point on the circle where it meets one edge of the plywood (or the drawn square), and draw a line from this point straight through the center of the circle. Measure and mark a point 13 inches (33 cm) down this line from the edge of the circle. Now measure and mark 13 inches (33 cm) from this same edge of the plywood (or square), but from the corner this time. Draw a line through these two points, perpendicular to the first line, and out to the edges of the circle. Where this perpendicular line intersects the circle are the two other points of the equilateral triangle. Draw the triangle by connecting the three points located on the circle. Draw two more lines from the center of the circle out to the two new points of the triangle. Finally, cut out the circle.

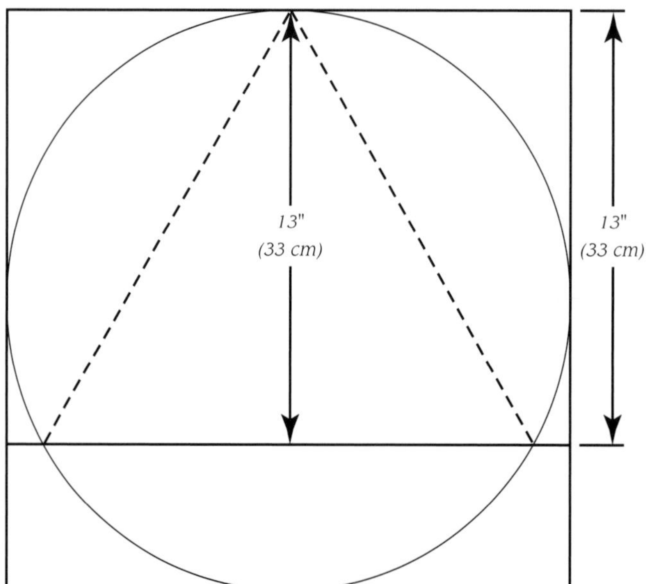

4. Position the three blocks of wood onto the plywood where the footstool's feet will go. Place each block so that the center point on the 2-inch (5.1 cm) end sits at one point of the triangle. Position each piece so that a line drawn down its center would extend through the center of the circle. Perfect alignment isn't critical; just use your eye to place the blocks. Then use wood glue to attach the three pieces into position.

5. When the glue has set, mark the points of the triangle on the edges of the plywood, and turn over the circle. Then extend the marks to the other side of the plywood, and draw another triangle by connecting these points. As you did on the first side of the plywood, draw lines from the three points through the center of the circle. (You'll have to reestablish the center point on this side of the plywood.)

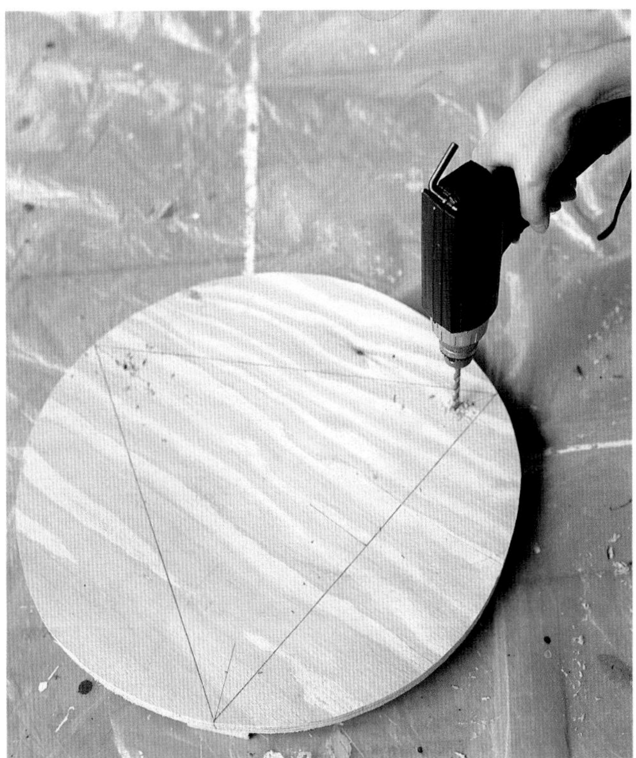

6. From each point in the triangle, along the line that intersects with the center point, measure and mark a distance that is half the diameter of the base of the wooden feet, about 1-1/2 inches (3.8 cm). With your plywood circle sitting on a piece of scrap lumber, drill a hole at each point, drilling all the way through the plywood and the wooden block. Make each tap hole the proper size for your wood screws, and try not to damage anything underneath. Then drill a hole through the center of the circle of plywood.

7. Now go to work on the foam. If you have two foam rounds, glue them together using the glue gun. Working a few inches at a time, apply the glue around the edge, and press the pieces together until the glue cools. Mark the center point on both sides of your 8-inch-high (20.3 cm) pillow.

8. To round the edges of the foam pillow, the top edge must be glued to the side of the pillow with cool-melt glue and the aid of a spring clamp. Using a straightedge and a ball-point pen, mark a line around the entire circumference on one of the rounds about 2 inches (5.1 cm) down from the top. The marked round will be the upper pillow. Begin to glue the top to the side by applying a short stream of glue just above the pen line and pressing the top edge into the side so that the edge aligns with the pen line. Hold the edge to the line for a few seconds until you can position the clamp to hold it together. Apply another stream of glue and proceed. Two clamps will speed up the process.

9. Thread the needle with 48 inches (122 cm) of upholstery twine. Use the marks you made in the center of both sides of the foam as guides to insert the long needle through the center of your pillow. Pull the twine through the tunnel made by the needle, and work the twine back and forth to enlarge the center hole so that you'll be able to locate it easily once the needle and twine have been removed. Then remove the needle and twine. Use the scissors to cut a funnel-shaped hole, bit by bit, about 3 inches (7.6 cm) wide and 2 inches (5.1 cm) deep in the top center of the foam. The gathered fabric will be pulled through this funnel partway into the center hole, so enlarge the top 1 to 2 inches (2.5 to 5.1 cm) of the center opening. Make small snips with the scissors to smooth out the funnel so that it's even and there are no big chunks cut out of the foam.

10. Attach the foam to the plywood base with the glue gun. The blocks of wood should be on the outside.

11. Before attaching the fabric to the stool, paint the ball feet. You can stain and seal the feet, and lightly sand them before adding opaque color splotches, or you can prime them and apply a base coat using the background color of the fabric.

12. Keep a swatch of your fabric where you can see it while you're mixing or selecting paints to match. To achieve the right color balance, it's also important to keep the swatch in view while you're painting. Start painting by making a few different but repeatable brush impressions on a piece of scrap wood. Choose the shape you like the best, and practice it to make sure that you can repeat it. Then, using the most dominant color in the fabric pattern, paint this shape on one foot. Keep repeating this shape on all three feet until the amount of color you have applied balances with the color in the fabric. Follow the same procedure for the other colors that you want to match in the fabric.

13. Before you cut the fabric to size, wrap it lengthwise around the plywood and foam circle to check for any problems with the lay of the pattern and weave. Cut the fabric to 18 by 60 inches (45.7 by 152.4 cm). Fold one of the short sides of the fabric under about 1 inch (2.5 cm), and begin to staple the lower edge of the 60-inch (152.4 cm) length to the side of the plywood base. Staple every 2 inches (5.1 cm) until you've come nearly all the way around the circle. Turn under the last 2 inches (5.1 cm) of the fabric, and overlap the beginning piece of fabric by about 2 inches, stapling the end tightly in position.

14. Thread the needle again with twine right off the spool. Don't cut the end of the twine; let it run off the spool. Thread the needle through the hole in the bottom of the plywood and through the tunnel in the foam. If you can't get the needle to reach all the way through, compress the foam until the needle surfaces and you can pull it through. Gather the top edge of the first 12 inches (30.5 cm) of the fabric into six 1-inch (2.5 cm) folds, and thread the needle through the center of these folds about 1 inch from the edge of the fabric. Insert the needle back through the foam tunnel, leaving the fabric and twine loose on the top side. Wrap the twine loosely around the dowel, allowing it to trail, and release more twine from the spool as you need it to go back through the tunnel and gather the next six folds of fabric. Repeat this procedure until all of the fabric has been threaded onto the twine. Take the end of the twine through the foam one last time, and exit at the bottom of the plywood. Leaving a short trailer, cut the twine.

15. Cut a 48-inch (121.9 cm) length of twine, and thread it through the needle to make a doubled thread 24 inches (61 cm) long. Tie a knot in the end, and slip the twine over the dowel to keep it from pulling all the way through the foam. Insert the needle through the tunnel in the foam, through the shank of the button, and back through the foam and plywood. Slip the knotted twine off the dowel, and tie it to the other end of the twine after you've cut it off the needle. Tape this knotted mass off to one side of the center hole in the plywood.

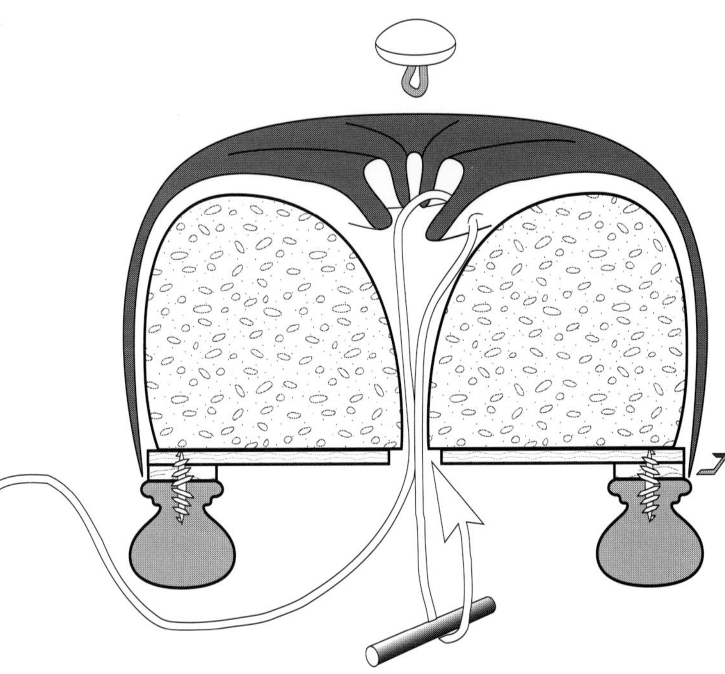

16. Gather together the three loops and two loose ends of the remaining twine. They've probably fallen off the dowel long ago. Tie the two ends together loosely around the dowel, slipping the loops over it too. Pull on the dowel to feed the fabric into the funnel-shaped hole in the foam. The goal is to pull all of the slack out of the twine, making the loops shorter and the tied twine ends longer, and at the same time, to feed more and more of the fabric into the tunnel.

17. Once you've fed all of the fabric into the beginning of the tunnel, turn the stool foam side down on a clean surface, and kneel on it. This will compress the foam and release more twine for you to pull. After you've gotten all of the slack out of the twine, tie a square knot in the end of the twine over the dowel, which is pulled tight to the base of the plywood circle. Wrap the twine several times around the dowel in a figure-eight pattern, and tie the ends again. Release the knotted twine that was taped out of the way, and pull it until the button is in position at the bottom of the funnel. Tie the ends of this twine securely around the dowel. To make sure all the knots stays secure, cover them with a layer of cool-melt glue.

18. The fringe that I selected for this stool was almost too short to cover the wooden blocks under the feet, so to make the blocks less obvious, they were brushed with white glue and covered with fabric before the ball feet were screwed into position.

19. Attach the trim with the glue gun, starting at the same spot where the fabric was started, and gluing over the staples. Use your finger as a guide to keep the trim the same distance from the edge all the way around. If you're applying more than one trim, you can do them all together with one turn of the stool by gluing one atop the other as you proceed. Butt the ends of the trim together, glue them securely, and finish with a cord bow glued on top.

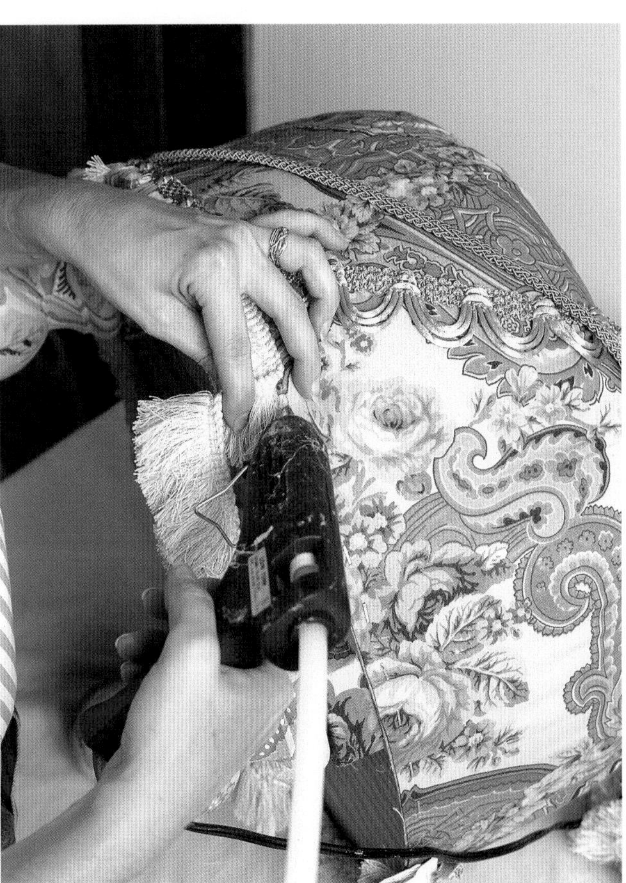

Restoring a Damaged Antique Cupboard

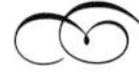

Liz and Pete Sullivan restore furniture professionally, and they have a real knack for repairing painted pieces. In this chapter they share some of their secrets for the removal of unsightly, flaking white paint that has been slathered over a handsome painted surface.

In its original state (see the photograph on page 128), I would have thought that this piece of furniture was irredeemable. The project repairs alone seemed too much for anyone to handle, but as I watched Liz and Pete tackle the various problem areas, I was pleasantly surprised. The difficulties seemed to melt away. When the project was complete, the rich color of the original milk paint was revealed and the authenticity of the cupboard preserved.

This cabinet, which was purchased for mere peanuts, could probably now be sold promptly and for a steep price by a New York antique dealer. Its countenance has retained all of the beautiful character lines of its past history, and it carries the lovely patina of age. The missing limbs have been replaced with vintage wood, and they were reglued and repainted with a dexterity and craftsmanship that defies surface detection. And they say that it's elementary!

If you have a similar painted piece that you want to restore, there's just one "secret weapon" that you must employ. The grimy, flaking white surface paint on this cupboard was removed with an electric hot-air gun. The gun allows you to remove layers of paint separately, while stripper removes every layer, including the original paint. These guns are readily available in hardware and paint supply stores.

Materials

- Project to be restored
- Scraps of wood with multiple layers of paint
- Paint and varnish remover
- Acrylic craft paints to match the original finish (those used here: midnight blue, Boston blue, Salem green)
- Wood the same thickness and similar grain as missing pieces, preferably aged
- Wood glue
- Scrap of cardboard for template
- 6d finishing nails
- Wood filler
- Accumulated pieces of removed paint, sawdust, and wood shavings
- Paste wax

Tools

- Tarpaulin
- Hot-air gun
- Putty knife with 1-1/2" (3.8 cm) blade
- Protective goggles
- Rubber gloves
- Old brush to apply stripper
- #3 steel wool
- Cotton or linen rags
- #120 garnet paper
- #4 round brush
- 2" (5.1 cm) flat brush
- Large clamps
- Pencil
- Saber saw
- Craft knife
- Hammer
- Nail set

Instructions

1. Before beginning any repairs, remove the doors and moldings where the pieces are missing.

2. It's important to save as much of the original paint as possible. The heat gun, with its ability to remove the paint layer by layer, is a good tool for this job, but perfecting the technique takes a little practice. Apply the heat to one of the scrap painted boards, holding the gun in one hand and the putty knife in the other. Keep the gun several inches from the surface, and your eye on the paint, watching it closely. As soon as you see the top layer of paint start to soften, gently lift it with the putty knife. Have patience; learning just how much time to leave the gun in one area takes practice. Once you feel that you've gotten the layer-by-layer paint removal system down pat, start working on your project in an unobtrusive place. You won't be able to remove all of the top layer or save all of the original paint—some spots will require touching up—but strip off as much of the top layer of paint as you can. Save the paint chips that fall onto the tarpaulin so that they can be used later.

3. The interior of this cabinet was stripped rather than scraped because it was originally unpainted; the white paint was added much later. To strip the interior, place the cabinet on its side. First strip one side; then flip the cabinet to reach the other side. With the cabinet flat on its back, strip the back of the interior and the shelves. The stripper is applied with an old brush and wiped off with steel wool and rags, according to the manufacturer's directions, while wearing protective eye and hand gear. Apply and remove the stripper twice to give the shelves and walls a scrubbed look.

4. When the wood is dry, sand the interior with the #120 garnet paper, and leave it dry, which in this instance means no varnish coat.

5. Touch up the original paint and any white spots on the cupboard exterior with the #4 brush and the appropriate color of acrylic craft paint (midnight blue for this project). For larger areas, smear on the paint with a clean cotton or linen rag.

6. While the paint is still wet, rub sawdust and dry paint chips into it.

7. When the paint is dry, brush away any loose residue of the chips and sawdust with a clean, dry flat brush.

8. The base on this cabinet was cracked and broken, as you can see in the picture of the cupboard before it was repaired. If your project has any bad cracks, glue and clamp them. Remove the base or other broken board, and use a saber saw to trim off the ragged broken edge so that another board can be easily glued and clamped to it to replace the missing portion. Before attaching the two pieces together, flop the old board, lay it face down on a piece of cardboard, and trace the outline. Then, using a craft knife, cut the pattern out of the cardboard. Cut the end of the new board to fit together with the old, but don't cut the rest of the shape yet. First glue and clamp the new board to the old. After the glue has dried, place the cardboard pattern over the new board, trace around the cardboard, and cut the board to shape with the saber saw. Finally, sand the joined pieces with the garnet paper to remove all sharp edges and traces of glue.

9. Nail the molding onto the base of the cupboard, setting the nails and filling the nail holes with wood filler. After allowing the filler to dry overnight, sand it smooth. Don't prime the fresh wood. To match the rest of the cabinet, simply smear on some of the acrylic paint with a rag. You can create a finish similar to this one by making patches of Boston blue and adding areas of Salem green and midnight blue, blending them together where they meet.

10. To give the paint an aged look, rub in some sawdust before the paint dries. This is an important antiquing trick to keep in mind for other projects as well.

11. Add a few more distress marks to the new paint, and sand off some of the edges. For more detailed information on distressing a painted surface, see pages 94–97.

12. To complete and protect the finish, rub paste wax onto the entire exterior surface of the cupboard.

Intarsia Painting on a Serving Tray

This is Marius. Like any self-respecting monkey, Marius has his own ideas about having his portrait painted. He doesn't want too much fuss, and he doesn't want to be kept too long from his more entertaining, playful pursuits. Fortunately for both him and me, capturing this delightful beast on wood is fairly easy and much less time consuming than you might expect.

It's done using a technique called intarsia painting, *which is very popular in Germany. Real intarsia is a mosaic worked in solid pieces of wood and is a process that requires dexterity and a high level of woodworking skill. Intarsia painting imitates the appearance of inlaid wood but is much simpler to do. With a pattern, craft knife, paint, and permanent marker, you can easily make a complex design.*

This image of Marius is an adaptation of the classic method. Traditional intarsia painting uses hard lines within the design to create the illusion of having several small pieces of wood inlaid together to make the mosaic. Without these lines, the portrait is more painterly and less like a mosaic, but the shading technique produces a glowing surface that suggests fine wood inlay.

Surrounding the portrait is a faux wood border that is an example of inlay painting. It mimics the practice of placing strips of veneer together on a diagonal so that they make a V where they come together in the center of each panel. It's easily produced by partially removing bands of glaze with a scumble brush.

The decorative corner squares are a little more difficult to paint only because of their tight quarters. These and the fanciful turquoise inlay add elegant touches that complement the luxurious color of the monkey's fur.

The globe is made from a photocopy of an image of the Earth photographed from outer space. You'll be able to find the same image in magazine advertisements and articles dealing with conservation and other environmental issues.

Materials

- Wooden tray
- Primer of your choice (see page 10)
- Acrylic craft paints: yellow, black, red, turquoise, white, mocha, old parchment
- Clear, self-adhesive plastic
- Pattern enlarged to fit your tray
- Fine-line permanent marker
- Photocopy of an image of Earth, sized to fit globe in pattern
- Adhesive solvent
- Water-based matte polyurethane
- Satin polyurethane
- 1" (2.5 cm) plastic, noncuring masking tape (see page 15)
- Burnt sienna artist's oil paint
- Mineral spirits
- Rectangular piece of thin cardboard

Tools

- #400 wet/dry sandpaper
- Craft knife
- Straightedge
- Pencil
- Ball-point pen with brightly colored ink
- Black carbon paper
- Artist's brushes: 1/2" (1.3 cm) scumble, 1/4" (6 mm) blunt end oil, 1/4" (6 mm) worn blunt end or scumble, #4 tapered point
- Cotton swabs
- Lint-free cotton rags
- Old toothbrush
- Pallet knife
- Small plastic spoon

Instructions

1. Before you start your project, trim the worn or inexpensive 1/4-inch (6 mm) brush to make a scumble brush by cutting straight across the bristles with a craft knife, leaving the bristles about 1/4 inch (6 mm) long.

2. Prime and sand the tray to a silky smooth finish. Then paint the tray with several coats of yellow paint, alternating the direction of each coat. Allow it to dry hard between coats, and wet-sand it very lightly with the #400 paper. Let the paint cure for five days.

3. On the surface of the tray, measure 1 inch (2.5 cm) in from the sides of the tray, and (with the pencil) draw a border all the way around. Continue each line all the way to the edges of the tray; the four lines will intersect, making squares in each corner. Now draw another line all the way around, 1/8 inch (4 mm) closer to the center of the tray and

parallel to the first line, making a second, thinner border. Finally, make a small mark to indicate the middle of these borders on all four sides.

4. Position, tape, and trace the small square pattern on all four corners using the carbon paper and ball-point pen.

5. The plastic self-adhesive sheeting used as a mask in this project has a glue on the back that is meant to cure over a short period of time. You don't want it to cure on your project because it will leave a sticky residue on the painted surface. If you use adhesive cleaner to lift the glue, the cleaner will damage the yellow acrylic paint. It's best to start this part of the project early on a day that you have free to devote to it.

With all this forewarning in mind, measure and cut a piece of plastic large enough to fit the bottom face of the tray. Remove the backing on the plastic, and apply it to the tray according to manufacturer's directions. Be sure to smooth it down from one end to the other, getting rid of as many bubbles as possible. Large bubbles can be pierced with a pin and the air forced out of them, but ignore the small ones once you have the plastic in position.

6. Position the pattern of Marius onto the tray surface, checking the horizontal alignment. The vertical center through his nose should line up with the center line in the top and bottom borders. Secure the pattern in position by placing the tape only at the top, as if it were a hinge. Tape the pattern to the wood surface, not to the plastic, and slide the carbon paper, face down, under the pattern. Using the ball-point pen, trace only the outline of the monkey, the globe, the stand, and the pillow onto the plastic. Then flip the pattern and carbon paper out of the way, but don't remove the tape.

7. With a fresh blade installed in your craft knife, cut along the pencil outlines. Then, using the straightedge as a guide, cut along the line that indicates the inside border.

8. Slide the point of the craft knife under the plastic to lift it, being careful not to damage the paint, and slowly peel away the plastic covering the background. Check the small areas between the bottom border and the monkey's legs to make sure that all the bits of plastic have been removed from the background.

9. Use the 1/2-inch (1.3 cm) brush and the black paint to daub in the background. Daubing is much like tamping—it's done with an up-and-down motion—but a lot more paint is applied. Apply the paint rather thickly.

10. When all of the paint is dry, remove the rest of the plastic. Then turn the pattern and carbon paper back into position on the tray, and trace all the details.

11. After removing the pattern, use the permanent marker to trace over all the lines.

12. Cut out the photocopy of the Earth, position it face down on the tray, and secure it with tiny pieces of tape. Dampen a cotton swab with the adhesive cleaner, and wet the back of the copy lightly. Don't allow the copy to move; wait a full minute before removing it. The image will have transferred to the tray.

13. Paint a coat of water-based varnish on the tray to seal it, allowing this to cure for at least 48 hours. Then sand it lightly with #400 paper and a little soapy water.

14. Mask the border with the noncuring masking tape.

15. Holding the clean rag folded comfortably in your hand, squeeze a 2-inch-long (5.1 cm) glob of burnt sienna paint straight out of the tube onto the cloth. Then wipe the paint evenly over the surface of the tray, covering all of the exposed yellow shapes with paint.

16. Use a clean cloth to remove excess paint and make an even sienna tone. Turn the rag often to an unused place, and wipe off the oil color selectively. Single out areas to highlight by wiping off a little more paint. For example, assuming that the light comes from the upper right corner, you should remove some paint to create a highlight on the monkey's elbow, the top of his tail, one side of his face, and one side of the globe. Use a folded edge of the rag over the tip of your index finger to remove the paint from small sections. Notice that you can get very soft shading with the cloth. You have plenty of time to work because the paint won't dry for quite some time. Stop removing paint any time you like. A lot of shading and detail isn't necessary. The more paint you leave, the more inscrutable Marius looks.

17. If you wipe away too much paint, then apply a little more with the rag or the 1/4-inch (6 mm) untrimmed brush. Use the same brush to enhance the shadows in the fur above his brow and on the left side of his nose.

18. Remove the masking tape from the border, and allow the paint to dry for several days. When the paint has dried thoroughly, mix 4 spoonfuls of sienna with 2 spoonfuls of mineral spirits. Fold the mineral spirits into the oil paint a drop at a time, mixing them together with a pallet knife.

19. Before painting the border, mask the main area of the tray with paper, and tape over the corners, the smaller inside border, and the inside edges of the tray sides. To prevent any leakage of paint, burnish down the edges of the tape where it abuts the border.

20. To make the graining pattern on the border, apply the glaze mixture to half of one section of the border with the 1/2-inch (1.3 cm) brush. Starting at the corner and working toward the center, create the graining with the 1/4-inch (6 mm) trimmed brush by wiping away some of the glaze every 1/4 inch (6 mm) at an angle of about 45 degrees. Use the rectangle of cardboard at the center line of the border to

mask the other half while you complete the diagonal lines at the center. When the other half of the section is completed, the graining will create a V in the center.

21. Work every other half-section of the border, and allow the paint to dry before graining the others. Then remove the masking tape, and let the tray dry for five days.

22. Mask the area around the corners, and paint in the design using the #4 brush and the mocha, red, and white acrylic paint. With the old parchment paint, apply a highlight along the center of the mocha-colored diagonal. Then paint the red silk cording over the top. Paint in the background with the black paint. When the paint dries, sharpen the image by outlining everything with the black marker. Again, let the paint dry.

23. Mask all sides of the narrow, inside border, burnishing the edges well. Then paint it with turquoise paint. After letting the paint dry, spatter it with a few specks of black paint. Dip the toothbrush into a little paint, and rub the bristles against the edge of a bottle cap to make the spatters.

24. Mask the face of the tray, and paint the sides inside and out with the same technique used on the wide border. Use any leftover glaze to paint the bottom of the tray.

25. One week later, apply three coats of satin varnish to the entire tray, lightly wet-sanding with the #400 paper between coats.

Traditional Folk-Art Bed

Down through the centuries and away from the centers of wealth and cathedral towns in Europe, a unique and lively art form evolved. Influenced by the colors, shapes, and lines of fine furnishings, folk artists developed a style of work that imitated the carvings and embellishments of the highly skilled artisans. These folk artists may not have been formally schooled or apprenticed to the masters, and their materials and pallet may not have been grand. Nevertheless, using the equipment and skills available to them, they created works of art that still, centuries later, sing out with life and the joy of their creation. The remoteness and isolation in which they worked gave their art a character all its own, which may be appreciated more today than when it was created.

Warm red, yellow ocher, grayed green, and black were often the colors used by these country artists, and the design on this cannonball bed was one of theirs.

I first admired this cannonball bed frame at an auction, where it was selling for an absurdly small sum. I didn't need a bed frame, but I had auction fever. Now I own the frame plus several other things that I don't need. I don't attend auctions anymore; there are too many bargains in need of a home.

This frame is dated 1925, which isn't too old to paint in good conscience and without concern for historical accuracy. It originally held its mattress on rope, which seems a very old style to me, and the support system actually inspired the selection of this decorative pattern, which is several centuries old. I originally saw this type of ornamentation on a country chair, and it could easily be adapted to work on a dresser or chest. Once the pattern was completed, the frame was finished with a glaze that simulates an aged appearance.

Materials

- Old bed frame or other project
- Primer of your choice (see page 10)
- Acrylic water-based paints or matte oil-based enamels: yellow ocher, red, olive green, black
- Pattern sized and traced in pencil onto tissue or parchment paper
- Masking tape
- Paint pens or watercolor pencils (optional): black, red, green
- Water-based satin polyurethane (with paint pens) or semi-gloss polyurethane, not water based (with watercolor pencil)
- Special walnut stain

Tools

- #400 wet/dry sandpaper
- 2" (5.1 cm) brush
- Ball-point pen with bright-colored ink
- Black carbon paper
- Plates, platters, and other circular or oval pieces to be used as guides
- Artist's brushes: #2, #4, and #6 rounds
- Clean rags

Instructions

1. The project that you've chosen to paint must first be properly prepared and primed according to the general instructions on pages 8–10. When the primer has dried thoroughly and has been lightly sanded with #400 paper and a little soapy water, you're ready to apply the first coat of yellow ocher. If you're unable to find yellow ocher, a water-based paint called antique gold will work well.

2. Apply several coats of ocher to achieve a smooth, even painted surface. Sand lightly after the second coat, taking care not to sand down to the primer. Continue to sand the dry paint every second coat. Multiple coats of ocher may be necessary to achieve an even, opaque base color.

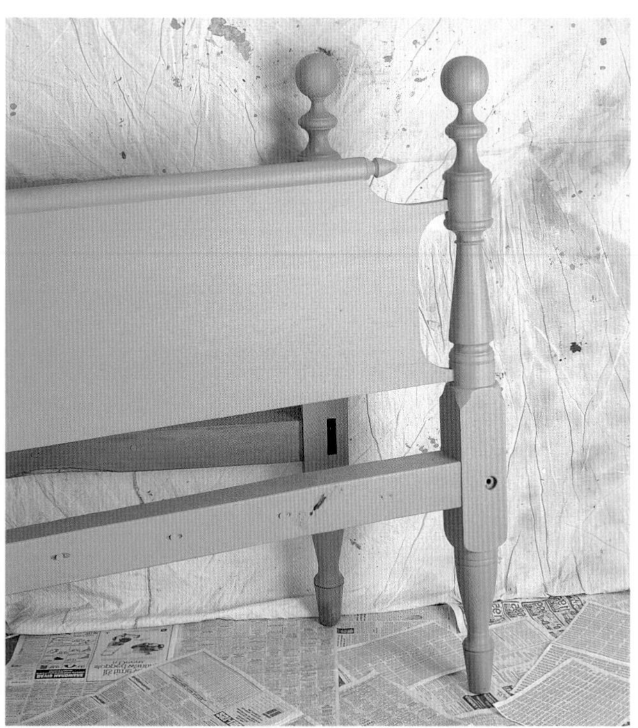

3. Once your base color has dried completely, determine the center of your headboard. Position and tape the tissue pattern on half of the board, and trace the pattern onto the board using the carbon paper, ball-point pen, and the plates or other oval or round shapes that you've chosen. Select the right shape and size of plate, place it on the pattern lines, and use it as a drawing guide to give you smooth, even lines.

4. When you finish tracing, flip the pattern back, and check your work before removing the tape and tissue. Now turn over the tissue so that the pattern covers the other half of the headboard, and follow the same instructions for tracing. Once you've completed the headboard tracings, do any smaller tracings on the bedposts before you begin painting.

5. The painting is done one color at a time. Start with the red, painting the headboard first, then the trim and details. If you have trouble painting a smooth curve, draw a guideline using your plates and a paint pen or red watercolor pencil. Then paint up to your guideline.

6. Loosen up by practicing with your brushes on some scrap paper, and get the feel of your brush working for you by varying the pressure you apply. Note how the weight of the line changes from fine to full brush width, and notice how many of the small shapes in this design are made entirely by placing the brush against the board and applying various amounts of pressure. Let your paintbrush do the work for you when it comes to thick and thin shapes and lines.

7. The green is the second color to be applied. When that paint is dry, reposition the tissue, and trace the areas that are to be painted in black.

8. Black is last color to be painted, which allows you to cover up any small errors. If you buy only one paint pen, this is the color to buy because it will be the most useful. Use the black paint pen to outline; then fill in with a brush and paint. If you're painting a curve free hand, keep your eye on your end point, not on the brush. This technique will give you a smoother, better flowing stroke and will help eliminate broken lines.

9. After your painted pattern has dried thoroughly, apply a coat of polyurethane to the entire bed. If you've used any paint pens, be sure to apply water-based polyurethane; otherwise, use the solvent-based finish.

10. After allowing this layer to dry overnight, wipe on the special walnut antiquing stain one area at a time using a small, soft, lint-free rag or 2-inch (5.1 cm) brush. Within

15 minutes, use a soft rag to wipe off the excess stain in the direction of the grain. Leave enough glaze to give the painted pattern an aged appearance. An alternative method is to pat off the glaze, starting in the center of the red spiral and working outward, leaving more stain on the outer edges.

11. Allow the stain to dry 24 hours; then apply two more coats of polyurethane.

Contemporary Folk-Art Cabinet

Historically, folk-art painted furniture was the product of Old-World artisans who reproduced the patterns and colors popular with a previous generation of aristocracy. Their work was simpler in design and considerably less expensive than the originals, for it was made for peasants and country folk. The American heritage of handmade and painted furniture has similar traditional roots, but it has evolved into an exuberant, contemporary art form. The warmth and whimsy expressed in this modern version of folk art is capable of lighting up a room and lifting your heart.

The best part about creating your own folk art is that the idea—not technical ability—is king. In fact, technical ability can often produce stilted results that lack honesty and character. To get in the mood, jump into your most frivolous self, grab a brush, scratch pad, and pencil. And remember, straight lines are out.

Any cabinet, table top, door front, even a refrigerator can be painted with the patterns shown here. If you don't have something on hand, antique shops and used furniture stores are often treasure-troves for inexpensive pieces.

In fact, I was scouring through a musty antique shop one gray afternoon, when I came across a very ugly little cabinet. It stood hiding behind some better-looking stuff that not even the local charity shop would bother to display. I walked on, saving my keen predatory eye for a more worthy treasure, but everything was dust and high dollar. "How much for this?" periodically rang through the murk, followed by a thunderous, ridiculous answer. Not even real antiques were that expensive! Then I heard a price that was music to my ears. I didn't care what the item was; I wanted it before another buyer could pounce on it. "I'll take it," burped out of my mouth, as I tumbled over my feet to see what I had claimed. I knew even before it came into view that it was that cabinet. Amazingly, as another shopper began showing some interest, the cabinet developed increasing charm in my eyes. I resolved that I wouldn't let anyone buy it out from under me; I had to have it!

You, of course, don't have a cabinet like this to paint, but the pattern can be adjusted to fit any project that you have available. If you're buying a cabinet to paint, keep in mind a few pointers: oak grain is especially difficult to paint over; whatever piece you choose should be sturdy; and don't paint over something that is valuable in its own right.

Materials

- Cabinet or other project
- White primer
- Acrylic paints: ultra blue, old parchment, terra cotta, black, white, yellow, red iron oxide, fire red, and small amounts of various colors
- Patterns enlarged to size and copied onto tracing paper
- Masking tape
- 3" x 3" x 1/4" (7.6 cm x 7.6 cm x 6 mm) balsa wood
- Rock-hard water putty
- Water-based matte varnish
- 1/4" x 1-3/4" (3 mm x 4.4 cm) round head bolt and nut
- Rubber washer to fit bolt

Tools

- Sanding block
- #100 garnet sandpaper
- Rags
- Tack cloth
- Foam applicators: 1" (2.5 cm), 2" (5.1 cm), and 3" (7.6 cm)
- Wet/dry sandpaper: #240, #320, and #400
- Straightedge
- Carbon paper
- Ball-point pen with bright-colored ink
- Paintbrushes: #2, #4, and #6 rounds; 1/2" (1.3 cm) and 1" (2.5 cm) flats
- Craft knife
- Pallet knife or dull kitchen knife
- 3-sided rubber graining comb
- Chalk
- Measuring tape
- #4/0 steel wool
- Drill and bit

Instructions

1. Remove any hardware, and sand all surfaces with the #100 paper. Sand just enough to scuff up the finish so that it will bond with the paint. (See pages 8–9 for additional information on sanding.) After sanding, wipe your project first with a rag, then with a tack cloth. With one of the larger foam applicators, apply two coats of white primer, first to the inside, then the outside of your cabinet. Sand with #240 paper between coats. White primer isn't always necessary on a lighter cabinet, but the blue color loses its intensity when painted over dark wood.

2. Map out your chosen locations for the various patterns using a straightedge and a pencil. On the dry and sanded cabinet, apply at least two coats of the blue paint inside and out, omitting those areas that call for a different colored background behind the birds and at the base of the cabinet. Sand lightly with #320 paper between coats.

3. Using the 1-inch or 2-inch (2.5 or 5.1 cm) foam applicator, paint two coats of old parchment in the rectangle behind the large hen, sanding between coats with #400 paper. Don't worry about butting the parchment color perfectly with the blue; you'll be covering the seam with a black line later. Just try to be relatively neat.

4. Once the paint has dried, position your pattern tissue, and secure it with small pieces of masking tape. Slide carbon paper under the tissue, and trace over your lines with a ball-point pen. After removing the tissue, paint the hen black, the straw and hen's beak golden yellow, the hen's comb and facial feathers red, and the egg white. The colors may seem bright, but a glaze will dull them later. When the hen is dry, give her a light sanding with #400 paper and a wipe with the tack cloth before adding another coat of paint. After the second coat has dried, you can add her white polka dots with the end of a small paintbrush dipped into the paint. Paint the eye white, and add a dot of black in the center.

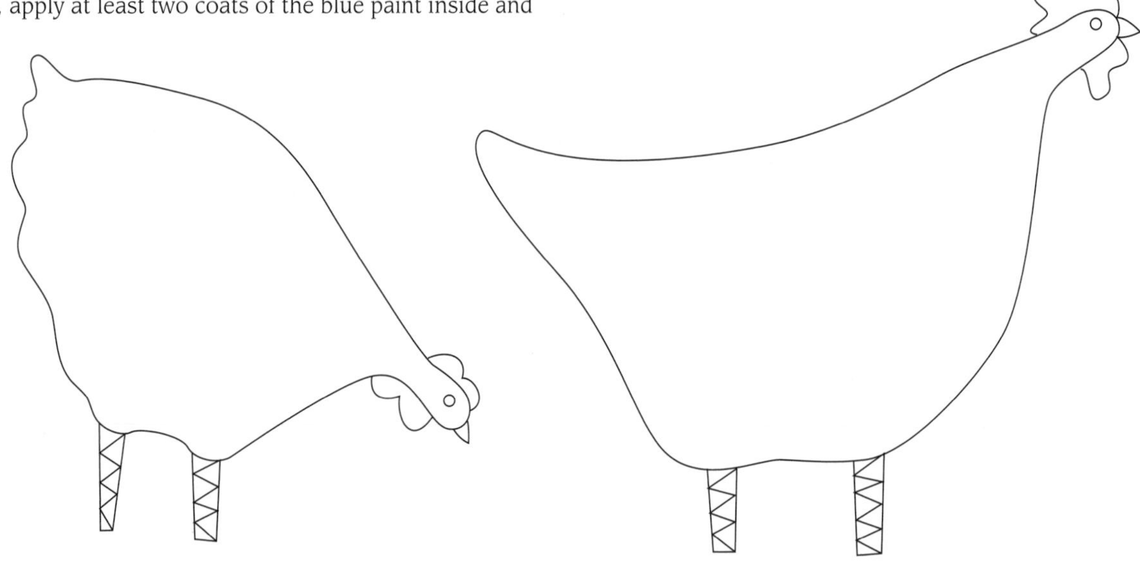

5. While your paint is drying, tape and trace the wing pattern onto the balsa wood, and cut out the wing with the craft knife. Mix up the water putty according to the manufacturer's directions (watch the water), and apply a 1/8-inch (3 mm) coat to both sides of the balsa wood using a pallet knife or a dull kitchen knife. If you don't coat both sides, the balsa will warp. Stand the wing on edge to dry. Then sand it smooth with #100 paper, and add another coat of putty. To help cut down on the sanding, the putty can be smoothed with a damp fingertip while it's in the process of drying. When you've sanded your second layer smooth, paint the wing with two coats of black, and add the white dots.

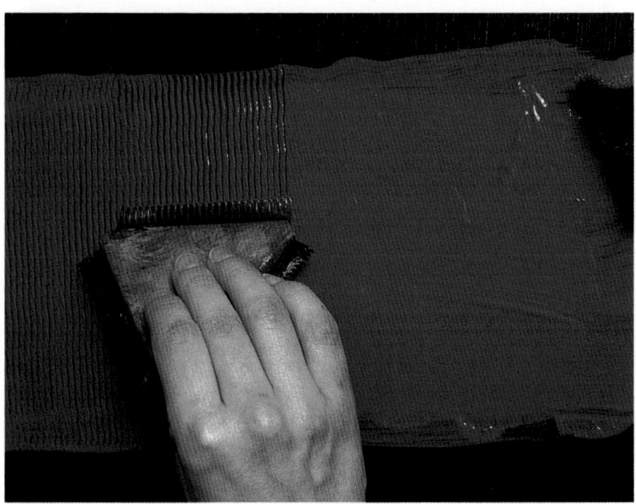

6. Paint the rectangle behind the four smaller chickens with a base coat of black, and let it dry. Working with one door or section at a time, apply the terra cotta paint. Then, holding the combing tool perpendicular to the surface with the rounded ends down, pull straight but firmly through the paint. A mistake can be wiped off, the area repainted, and the combing started again. Wipe the comb clean of paint, align the teeth in the last row made by the comb, and repeat the process using each preceding row as a guide line until the panel is finished. The same procedure is repeated on the bottom section of the doors.

7. When the combed paint is dry, trace and paint the chicks using the same methods and procedure used for the large hen.

8. Chalk is magical; it disappears when covered with paint, and it's gone without a trace after a damp sponge passes over it. It's perfect for drawing a design onto a surface that's already been painted. Use your chalk to draw lines indicating where you want decorative borders: around the rectangles, around the door edges, and around any additional spots that are in need of embellishment.

9. Anywhere that you're going to put a patchwork border should be painted in black first. Paint the chalk areas using the 1/2-inch (1.3 cm) brush. Keep it fairly well loaded with paint to avoid ragged edges and that lack-of-conviction look.

10. Next use your chalk to draw the decorative circles that appear all around the edges of the cabinet doors. Remember, after all that I've said about folk art, don't

make them perfectly round. Paint them using the same 1/2-inch (1.3 cm) brush. Start with various light colors of your choice. Place the brush in the center of each circle, press down, and twist it between your fingers to swirl it around. The ends of the bristles will give you a nice crisp edge. When the first layer dries, add a concentric circle of color with a #4 brush, then another and another until there is no room left. Use bright colors, since they will be glazed over with a dark wash.

11. Another chance for fun and unselfconscious expression begins with the chalking-in of the little bits of patterned charm scattered in the black borders over the cabinet doors. You can look closely at the patterns used here and copy them, or check around your home and collect a few motifs of your own. Mark the patterns on the door fronts over the black paint. These marks are just a guide, so stay loose. Start painting the patterns using the #4 brush and any color that strikes your fancy. Add smaller details with the #2 brush. Again, relax and enjoy the process.

12. Now that you have painted the patterns and have them where you want them, stand back, squint, and take an objective look at your work. Does it need more decoration? If it doesn't look quite right to you, add more. With folk art, more of a good thing is always better.

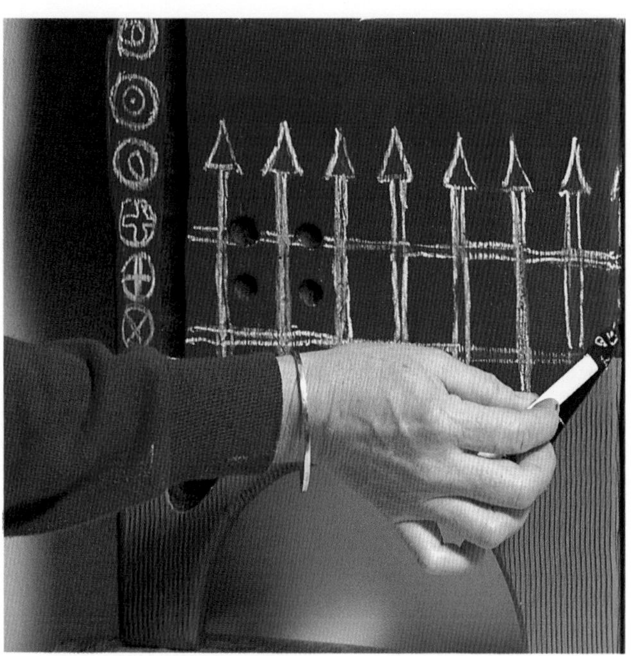

13. The fence is chalked on next. Measure and make tick marks where you want the verticals to go. The spacing should be planned to come out even. Chalk a horizontal line across the top to indicate the height of the fence posts. Use the 1/2-inch (1.3 cm) flat brush and the red iron oxide paint to do the fence. Place the brush at the top horizontal line and draw the brush down as straight as you can, keeping the tip of the brush flat against the surface. Do all the posts the same way. When the paint is dry, chalk the indications for the horizontal cross members and the fence post tops. Paint in the horizontals with the 1/2-inch (1.3 cm) brush and the tops with the #4 brush.

14. Several days of drying time later, you're ready to tame the colors of your cabinet. Those who prefer brightness to subtlety can add one or two coats of a clear matte varnish, and skip the glaze. Otherwise, mix a rather large amount of glaze. This cabinet required a total of 11 ounces (325.6 ml): 8 ounces (236.8 ml) of matte varnish mixed with 2 ounces (59.2 ml) of black, and 1 ounce (29.6 ml) of raw umber. Stir the mixture well but gently. The large amount of glaze is your insurance against color matching problems.

15. Wipe the cabinet first with a rag, then with the tack cloth. Apply the glaze to the entire cabinet using the 3-inch (7.6 cm) foam applicator. Start with the inside; then glaze the shelves and the exterior. Save the doors for last.

16. By the time you get to the doors, you should have a pretty good feel for how the glaze flows and just how long you have before it gets too tacky to spread. You may need to add water to make the job easier. Before starting the doors, rub them lightly with #4/0 steel wool. Then give them a good dusting off and a very thorough wipe with the tack cloth. If you're the least bit nervous about achieving an even coat of glaze, guard your treasured art work on the doors by applying a clear coat of matte varnish before glazing. Apply the glaze to the doors with the 3-inch (7.6 cm) applicator. Also apply a coat to the wing door closure.

17. After reattaching the hardware on your cabinet, drill a hole in the wing where it's indicated on the pattern. Position the wing in a convenient location on the cabinet door, and mark the location of the hole on the door. Once you've drilled the hole, attach the wing with the round head bolt, washer, and nut.

18. Coat the entire cabinet with clear varnish.

Faux Rosewood Cabinet

The beauty of rosewood is equalled only by the atmosphere of richness that it creates in a room. The grain is lush and the character unmistakable. With the depletion of the world's tropical rain forests, rosewood has become more rare and yet more highly treasured. Fortunately, by duplicating the graining with paint, we can have the beauty of this rosy wood grain in our homes without destroying a single rare tree.

This piece of furniture was purchased from a store specializing in unfinished pine furniture. This purchase taught me a harsh lesson. Before accepting a piece of unfinished furniture, check it over very carefully. Do the doors close snugly and lay flush against the main box? Is the wood free of deep saw marks? Is the routing perfectly even and correctly joined? Does the molding meet at the correct 45-degree angle and fit together tightly? Are there any exposed nails? It's amazing how much made-to-order unfinished furniture can differ from the showroom samples. On this piece, the door panels and part of the door framing were a disaster.

The method described here for painting this inexpensive pine cabinet with rosewood graining is simple, and the results are relatively quick and gratifying. The textured finish on the door panels is just as easy to achieve, and it makes a quick fix for damaged panels that would take too much elbow grease to repair. It would also make an interesting faux slate for a table top.

The inspiration for the method of dealing with the poorly crafted doors and the images to go on them came from my mental image of a service, which is called the blessing of the animals, held once a year at a local church. I've never seen the actual event, but as I understand it, the members of the church bring all kinds of animals, from llamas to frogs, to this special blessing service. There are miniature horses, goats, chickens, fish, dogs, and cats, all stuffed into a little downtown church with the rest of the congregation.

I wish I could have been there to see the animals and their people as the program progressed: frogs escaping from pickle jars; children wailing until a stray lizard is recovered; cockatiels trilling along to the soul-raising hymns; chickens plucking hungrily at the women's headgear; and the minister, with his spiritual countenance so full of warmth and kindness, standing unruffled through all this mingling of flesh, fur, and feathers. With these and other thoughts about this unique service in my head, I decided to paint the blessed beasts tracking their way home for the evening meal after a day spent in God's church, the Earth.

Materials

- Cabinet or other project
- Primer of your choice (see page 10)
- Artist's oil paints: alizarin crimson, burnt sienna, vermillion hue or toluidine red, white, raw umber, burnt umber, Prussian blue
- Cobalt drier
- Turpentine or mineral spirits
- Orange shellac
- Gloss polyurethane, small amount
- Semigloss polyurethane
- Facial tissue
- Water-based sealer, glue, and finish
- Acrylic craft paints: old parchment, mocha, black
- Pattern sized for your cabinet

Tools

- Medium and fine sandpaper
- Sanding block
- Clean, lidded containers for mixing
- Pallet knife
- Plastic teaspoon (5 ml)
- Artist's brushes: 3" (7.6 cm) blunt end, 2" (5.1 cm) blunt end, 1" (2.5 cm) blunt end, 1/2" (1.3 cm) blunt end, #6 badger with original protective sleeve, #4 round, #4 fan
- #400 wet/dry sandpaper
- #4/0 steel wool
- Ball-point pen with bright-colored ink
- Carbon paper
- Bucket
- Synthetic sponge
- Clean, soft cloth

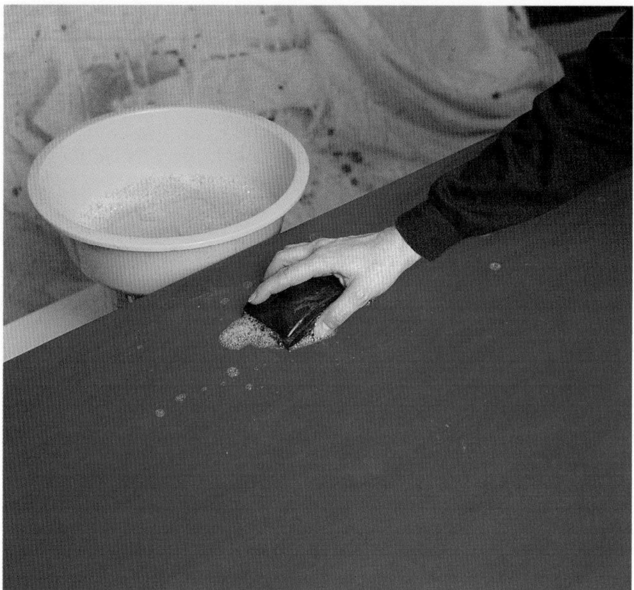

Instructions

1. Before starting to paint, fill all holes and correct any imperfections as much as possible. Sand the project, prime it, and sand it again.

2. Mix the paint for the base color of the rosewood in a clean container with a tight-fitting lid. Blend together 1 teaspoon (5 ml) of white, 8 teaspoons (40 ml) of alizarin crimson, 5 teaspoons (25 ml) of burnt sienna, and 2 teaspoons (10 ml) of vermillion hue or toluidine red. Use the pallet knife to fold the oil paint together, mixing until you have one solid color. Add 2 teaspoons (10 ml) of drier, a drop at a time, working it in with the pallet knife. Then dribble in turpentine or mineral spirits, mixing with the pallet knife to make a smooth liquid that is as thick as syrup.

3. Apply this mixture to the cabinet with the 2-inch (5.1 cm) brush, brushing in the direction of the grain.

4. Allow the paint to dry well between coats, and lightly wet-sand it with soapy water after the second coat. It may take three or more coats of paint to cover the primer well. Wet-sand it again after the last coat of paint.

5. Apply two coats of shellac to the dry and lightly sanded paint. When the shellac is dry, you're ready to start the graining.

6. Following the same blending method used for the reddish base color, mix together 8 teaspoons (40 ml) of raw umber, 4 teaspoons (20 ml) of burnt umber, 2 teaspoons (10 ml) of Prussian blue, 1 teaspoon (5 ml) of drier, and 1/2 cup (118 ml) of gloss polyurethane. If you need to thin this graining mixture to get it to a more spreadable consistency, add mineral spirits a dribble at a time.

7. Paint a stripe of the glaze on the cabinet from top to bottom using the 1/2-inch (1.3 cm) brush and a firm but light stroke. Don't try to make the stripe straight. Natural jiggles and bumps will make the graining more convincing, and you should add a few if they don't happen naturally.

8. When you've completed the stripe, use the badger brush to tamp one side of the stripe line to soften it. Position the plastic sleeve close to the end of the bristles to add firmness to the brush, and tamp with an up-and-down motion and not much more pressure than the weight of the brush itself. Soften only one side of the stripe.

9. Dip a fan brush into the graining mixture, and run it down the softened side of the stripe, echoing any bumps or jiggles in the striped line.

10. When the fan brush runs out of paint, refill it, and continue where you left off. This will leave a mark that you can disguise with the badger brush and a little more tamping. Where you have a mark, mute it by tamping on a diagonal slant, using the same up-and-down motion that you used to soften the edge of the stripe.

11. With the #4 round brush, touch up any other smaller flaws where the grain lines don't flow together smoothly.

12. Finish the entire cabinet using this procedure. Allow the glaze to dry thoroughly; then rub it *very* lightly with the soapy water and the #4/0 steel wool. Make sure the surface is dry and clean before applying two coats of semigloss polyurethane, wet-sanding between coats.

13. The slatelike finish on the door panels is created with facial tissue and a commercially prepared water-based sealer, glue, and finish product. First paint the sealer on the raw wood surface with the 1-inch (2.5 cm) blunt-end brush. Then place a single layer of facial tissue (use just one ply of a two-ply tissue) on the sealer, brushing it into position with the sealer-coated brush.

14. Repeating this procedure, place another single sheet of tissue so that it's butted against the first sheet on the wet surface. Then coat the second sheet with sealer.

15. When the first layer is complete, apply a second layer of tissue onto the wet sealer, staggering the seams with those in the first layer. Again, add a coat of sealer overall.

16. Once the sealer is dry, apply a coat of parchment paint to the panels, taking care not to get it on your glowing rosewood. After the parchment paint has dried hard, apply a layer of mocha paint. Before the mocha can dry, lightly wipe it off with a barely damp sponge, leaving mocha in the depressions and in the corners to create a halo effect. Allow this paint to dry.

17. Position the pattern on the tissue panels, adjusting the length to fit the proportion of your door by taking small tucks in the pattern sections where the tree trunks are located. Tape the pattern, leaving room to slip a piece of carbon paper underneath.

18. With the carbon side facing down on the door panel, trace the entire pattern with the ball-point pen. Repeat the procedure on the opposite door. Remove the patterns after checking to make sure the complete pattern has been traced.

19. Paint the tracing using the #4 brush and the black paint. Allow the paint to dry five days before using a clean cloth to wipe on a coat of semigloss polyurethane mixed with an equal portion of mineral spirits.

20. The bottom doors of this cabinet are a reflection of the same pattern used on the top two doors. Flop the pattern end to end, and trace, paint, and finish it using the same procedure.

Faux Marble Table with a Trompe l'Oeil Top

Faux marble painting is a lovely method of decoration that has been used by artists and craftsmen for almost 3,000 years. Still in existence today are some exquisite examples of marbling from ancient Egypt.

The translucent quality of polished marble draws the appreciative eye of the artist and almost begs to be imitated. In the past, creating faux marble was especially popular with those in colder climates where the stone itself wasn't easily accessible. Marbling was also used on pieces of furniture that already had portions of their anatomy carved from the real thing. Painting the legs to match a marble top saved money as well as decreased the overall weight of the piece.

The ability of oil-based paint to appear both opaque and translucent is similar to the character of natural marble. It's this very quality, along with a relatively slow drying time, that allows even an amateur to have easy success when creating a marble texture. The process isn't time consuming. Each layer of paint is applied to a wet surface, with one step following close on the heels of the last and with no delays or varnishes between layers. The most difficult aspect to bear is the time spent waiting for the painted finish to dry before proceeding with the next side of your project. If you choose not to wait for one side to dry, you risk damaging your completed surface.

I chose yellow marble for this table because it's a color that fits comfortably in almost any room. If you're going to use this technique on walls or other large areas, you may wish to soften the yellow ocher base color by diluting the glaze with more mineral spirits.

This technique for painting yellow marble has many applications. A dated-looking dining table could be a real scene stealer with a heavily varnished faux marble top and a natural or glazed wooden base (see pages 29–30 for instructions on glazing). The wood trim on a fireplace, a small jewelry box, canvas place mats, a lamp base, and a terra cotta urn are just a few of suggestions. If you change the base color from ocher to a melon shade created with rose madder paint, the possibilities multiply further.

The top of this table would have been lovely finished in wavy clouds of delicate amber marble, but that would have deprived me of the pleasure of presenting you with one last trompe l'oeil challenge.

Trompe l'oeil is a term for a visual illusion or painting done with such fine detail and accurate spatial relationships that the eye (oeil) tricks the brain into believing that the painted objects are real three-dimensional forms. The deception is complete and the artist's efforts rewarded when a viewer attempts to pick up one of the painted objects. Most of the faux finishes in this book, including faux marble, fall into the general category of trompe l'oeil.

There are various degrees of trompe l'oeil. Some are entertaining, conceptual paintings that don't intend to fool the eye but seek to amuse the viewer by suggesting that it can be done. Others are very sophisticated efforts done by talented professionals.

This table top is painted with a degree of trickery that lies somewhere between the conceptual and the master stroke. Although some items on this table aren't painting assignments for a beginner, the few easy techniques required for the beads, book, and doily are easily mastered by a novice. Instructions for the malachite finish that's used on the pen can be found on pages 88–90.

Trompe l'oeil objects are usually chosen for wit and because they're associated with the person who owns the piece of furniture on which the illusion is painted. All of the objects on this table are memorabilia or symbols of things that are significant in my life. Select a few items from your own possessions that are similar to these, and substitute. The directions and the tips that follow should give you all the necessary instructions.

Materials

- Table or other project
- Tinted cream-colored primer of your choice (see page 10)
- Artist's oil paints: yellow ocher, raw umber, burnt umber, French ultramarine blue, white
- Cobalt drier
- Mineral spirits
- Several pieces of crumbled newspaper
- Semigloss polyurethane, not water based
- Water-based satin polyurethane
- Trompe l'oeil materials and tools:
  - Book - 14 k gold gleams and maroon acrylic craft paints, black oil paint, fine mist spray bottle, toothbrush, masking tape, scrap paper, textured paper towel, gold paint pen
  - Beads - light pink, white, and various other colors of acrylic craft paints
  - Doily - white and gray acrylic craft paints, pencils with erasers, craft knife

Tools

- Pallet knife
- Plastic teaspoon (5 ml)
- Clean container for mixing
- Artist's brushes: 2-1/2" (6.4 cm) flat blender, 1" (2.5 cm) flat, 1/4" (6 mm) flat, #6 fan blender, #2 round, #4 round
- Sharp-pointed feather, at least 4" (10.2 cm) long
- Straightedge
- Circle guides

Instructions

1. Prepare your table or other project for painting by priming it in a cream color and sanding it smooth.

2. Marbling is done on one side of the table at a time, and on each side of the table, all of the steps in the marbling process must be completed while the glaze and all of the other layers of paint are still wet. It's best to allow the marbling plenty of time to dry before turning the table and continuing with the next side.

3. Mix the yellow glaze by adding 1 teaspoon (5 ml) of cobalt drier, a drop at a time, to 8 teaspoons (40 ml) of yellow ocher. Use the pallet knife to fold the drier into the paint. Then mix in 2 teaspoons (10 ml) of mineral spirits, a bit at a time, until all three elements are completely blended. Using the 1-inch (2.5 cm) brush, paint one side of the table with the glaze. Be sure to glaze the inside edges as well.

4. Use the 1/4-inch (6 mm) brush and some raw umber slightly diluted with mineral spirits to paint trailing diagonal lines through the wet ocher glaze.

5. Holding a crumpled piece of newspaper in both hands, roll the newspaper over the glazed surfaces with enough pressure to create crackled impressions in the glaze.

6. Use the dry 2-1/2-inch (6.4 cm) blender brush to soften the surface by *lightly* dragging it across the glaze in short 1-inch strokes. With the 1/4-inch brush and the diluted raw umber, create more defined veins across the surface of the glaze. Use the tip of the brush for this procedure, twisting it slightly between your thumb and forefinger to vary the thickness of the vein. Paint a diagonal main vein, and form narrower branches that travel in the same direction as the main vein. Paint small connecting veins very near the apex of the branches and the main vein.

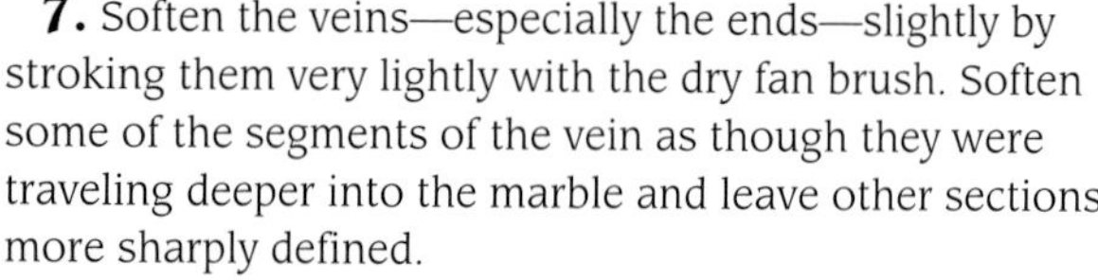

7. Soften the veins—especially the ends—slightly by stroking them very lightly with the dry fan brush. Soften some of the segments of the vein as though they were traveling deeper into the marble and leave other sections more sharply defined.

8. Apply lighter, fainter, and shorter veins with a scant amount of diluted French ultramarine blue. These veins should be only 2 to 3 inches (5.1 to 7.6 cm) long and should be blended to a very soft appearance with the fan brush.

9. Use the tip of the feather and the white paint to create short, unsoftened veins that cross the others.

10. After allowing the paint to dry, repeat the procedure on the other three sides. The inside surfaces of the legs should be done with the same care. Marbling always draws the viewer closer to touch the cool looking surface—the ultimate compliment—and you don't want any unfinished areas to mar the perception. Let the paint dry and cure before completing the illusion of polished stone by applying two coats of semigloss polyurethane.

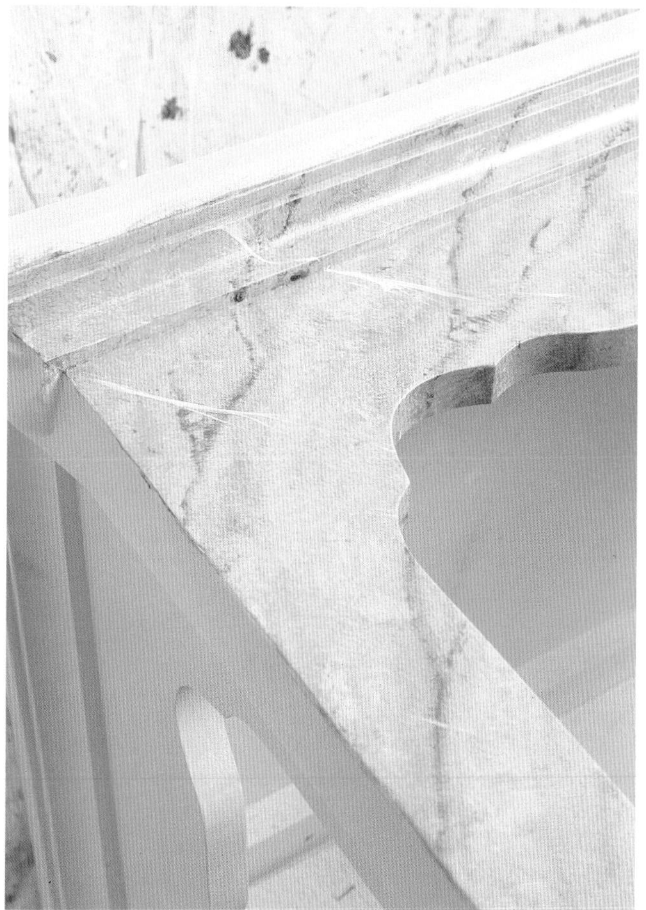

11. The trompe l'oeil images are painted on a cream base color that is silky smooth and finely sanded. Before you begin painting your trompe l'oeil masterpiece, here are a few tips that might be helpful.

- Choose items that have simple shapes and are shallow in depth. Objects with free-form shapes are the least difficult. The odd-shaped beads in this necklace are easy to do.
- Paint actual objects, and keep the object that you're painting right next to you while you work. Place the light source on the object so that you can see the effects you're reproducing.
- Arrange the objects on the surface that you're going to paint, light it the way you want to paint it, and take a picture from directly overhead. This photograph will help you see the relationships between objects while you're working on each one. In addition, you can have a full-size photocopy made from the print to use as a pattern. If you have a slide, you can project it onto the painted surface and trace the outlines of your objects.
- Reduce a complex object to its geometric parts. This book cover, for example, is made up of two triangles, a long rectangle, and a pentagon.
- Apply one color on top of another instead of butting one against the other. Observe an object carefully, and analyze the layers of color. These beads have a base color of pink, a slightly darker center of grayish pink over that, and a white highlight on top. The fish is first painted in gold, and the other colors are added on top.
- Use tape to mask your painting on straight edges whenever possible for a really sharp, realistic look.
- Develop all of the steps for painting an object before you begin.

12. To paint the small leather-bound volume, start by positioning the book on the table and tracing lightly around it with a pencil. Remove the book and sharpen the outlines by drawing over the lines using a straightedge and, for the slight curve at the end of the spine, the circle guide. Tape off the entire rectangle, burnishing the edges of the tape well to ensure a sharp edge to your paint.

13. With the 1-inch (2.5 cm) brush, apply a coat of the gold paint to the entire rectangle, making sure to follow the slight curve at the ends of the spine.

14. Allow the paint to dry. Then measure the leather trim, and draw its boundaries in pencil onto the gold rectangle. After masking the area around the leather trim, use the 1-inch (2.5 cm) brush to paint the trim with the maroon acrylic paint. While the paint is still wet, press a sheet of uncreased paper towel into the wet paint to simulate the texture of leather. Remove the paper towel, and allow the paint to dry.

15. Mask the off the gold area in the center of the book, using scrap paper to cover the rest of the table top. Make the glaze for this part of the book by mixing some black oil-

based paint with a little mineral spirits until you obtain the consistency of syrup. To apply the glaze, spritz the exposed area with a fine mist of water, and speckle the glaze onto the surface. Dip a toothbrush into the glaze, and press it against the edge of a jar or cap to deliver the spots of paint. Make larger spots by dipping the brush in the black syrup and tapping it lightly against a stick held over the wet surface.

16. Allow the speckled finish to dry before removing the tape. Finish the details of the book by first indicating the position of the gold embossing with a pencil and straightedge. Then go over the pencil lines with the gold paint pen. The curved spine is done with a thin wash of the gold paint, leaving gaps in the wash to indicate decorative embossments in the leather.

17. Draw the round beads lightly in pencil using a circle guide. Then paint a base color wash with a fine-tipped brush. After the base color has dried, apply washes of other decorative colors. Lastly, add a white highlight.

18. To paint a doily, lay the original in position on the table top, and trace the outline lightly, without applying any pressure to the edge of the crochet. Then paint the outlined area with white. Using a craft knife, cut the end of an eraser into the shape of the holes in the doily. Dip the eraser in gray paint, and stamp the shape onto the painted doily to form a lacy effect. The shadow of the book and cup are added later.

19. When you've completed all of the painting on the table top, allow the paint to cure for five days. Finish the project by applying several coats of satin polyurethane.